FLAVA MYPLATE

HE
HERBAN-EATS.COM

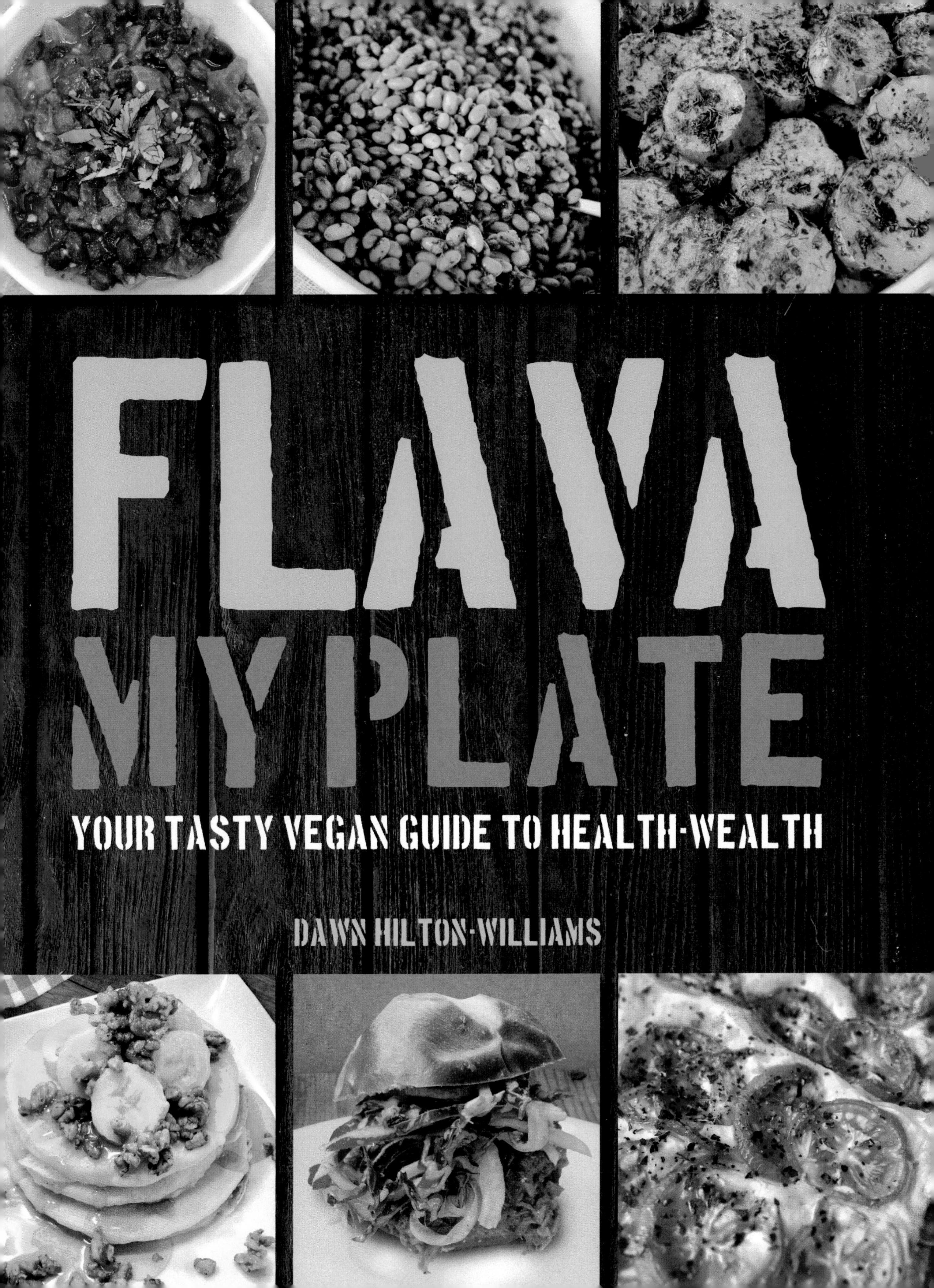
FLAVA
MYPLATE
YOUR TASTY VEGAN GUIDE TO HEALTH-WEALTH
DAWN HILTON-WILLIAMS

Flava my Plate is dedicated to my mother, Sandra, my husband, Anthony, Nadia and Kennedy.

Anthony, your support of every one of my dreams has never wavered and I can't put into words how rare and beautiful a thing that is; thank you! Nadia and Kennedy; you, and other millennials like you, will be the ones to put an end to the normalization of the needless practice of animal agriculture, food deserts, food bias and inequities, global warming/ climate change and preventable chronic diseases! Nadia thanks for sharing the journey with me as my daughter and remember to always unapologetically be who you are. To my mother-in-law, Brenda, thanks for your kindness and unwavering support; Anthony must have picked that trait up from you. To my mother, Sandra, too many things to thank you for and not enough space to rightly express the depth of my gratitude; thank you.

ACKNOWLEDGMENTS

Thanks Curtis and Tammie Miller of Maranatha Farms Community Supported Agriculture (CSA), for sharing your affordable, organic, goodness with the community. Thanks to all the beautiful children whose images, at Maranatha Farms, grace the pages of this book – you are, without question, our greatest why. Thanks Yvette for teaching me to find the image within pictures, much love to Patrice for always being more sister than cousin in every meaningful way. Special thanks to my Hilton and Williams family as well as the army of good friends who have contributed with encouragement and support.

Thanks to two of Herban-Eats' best cooking class students, Jackie Williams Hagood and Jimetta Littlejohn, as well as my daughter, Nadia, for sharing your bright smiles on the back cover, Paul Palmer-Edwards for the brilliant and creative book and cover design work and Robbie, Patrice, Sandra, Timaree, Kerri, and Mateel for your priceless review contributions.

A special thanks to Milton Mills, MD and Sunil Pai, MD for contributing quotes in support of this book and meaningful action in support of community in your everyday work!

To my Creator (God): I'm always grateful for the tasks and ready to do the work you've assigned. When what I do is helpful in the service of others, it affirms that I am operating within purpose. Thank you for the opportunity to listen, learn, evolve and serve.

Maranatha Farm Youth and Blue Truck Portrait Photography: Tammie Miller
Food Photography: Dawn Hilton-Williams
Book and Cover Design: Paul Palmer-Edwards
ISBN: 9780578453293

CONTENTS

PREFACE

The Beginning: Fertile Ground

The seeds of health-curiosity were firmly planted early on as I experienced the untimely loss of my grandparents. Like dominoes, my naïve childhood ideas about family and forever fell one after the other, each time I bore witness to the sudden haste or painful longsuffering of another relative making their transition. Bitter about what I deemed the unique unfairness of my familial circumstance, it became apparent that I wasn't alone because the vast majority of my friends were also grappling with the same experiences. Like an awful rite of passage, diagnoses for everything from hypertension, heart disease and diabetes to cancer, dementia and stroke were expected and accepted.

For the few elders in my family that didn't experience sudden death, I watched them all languish in hospitals and nursing homes choking down fistfuls of pills, as lidded trays filled with chronic disease-promoting foods rolled in and out of every room. Sadly, everyone I knew had built up a kind of unspoken immunity to the regularity of untimely death and like them, I adjusted to the awful ebb and flow of it all.

Growing up in a world where funerals were more frequently and better attended than family reunions, I looked grimly forward to saying my goodbyes and my hellos at each homegoing. Like a menacing plague, chronic disease wiped out more than 75% of my family before my teens and not once did I consider watering those neglected health-curiosity seeds planted in my soul garden all those years before.

Wake Up Call

My first five-alarm blaze roared on the scene in my late 30's, when I lost my father to a massive heart attack, complications from type 2 diabetes and congestive heart failure. The ransacked condition of his otherwise tidy bedroom and his lifeless body awkwardly strewn across the floor let me know that the fight for his last breath was a violent and painful one and all I wanted to know was why?

A caterer by trade, the months prior to my father's death led me more frequently to raising the unwelcome topic of healthier food choices and the occasional delivery of, what I believed then to be healthy options. Unfortunately, it was too little, too late. It was the river of tears from his passing and the unshakeable trauma that seeing him strewn across the floor left behind, that first flooded the soil around my parched seeds. Only after his transition did I make an earnest attempt to try and examine family deaths, chronic disease and what role, if any, food had to play.

Sitting down with the elder family I had left, I tried connecting any common health dots that might have led to a plausible explanation for so many untimely deaths. Unfortunately, those conversations were as unyielding as they were brief; leading most back to the easy conveyance of ideas like heredity, old age or God calling His children home. Unconvinced, I turned to internet search engines, libraries and bookstores to find some correlation between chronic disease and food but with so much conflicting data, my head was spinning like a top. What was true in one source was untrue in another and what worked for one group, was negated by another; it was exhausting!

With no definitive answers, it wasn't long before I was back to my presumed-healthy way of living. Back to depriving water for my newly growing health-curiosity seeds and back to normalizing untimely deaths like a seasoned pro. Like so many, I accepted the idea that what I was doing with food and lifestyle was far better than what my relatives had done and that would probably be just enough to break the back of the chronic disease reaper that terrorized my family.

Close to Home: The Heart and Cancer Scares

A former NCAA Division I football Athlete, my husband Anthony appeared to be the picture of health, but appearances, in this case, were deceiving. The first real sign of trouble was the high cholesterol report from his annual physical, which was shortly followed by complaints about heart flutters. After scheduling an appointment with a cardiologist, I spent a good deal of time wondering, "how could this be?'' All the eggs I purchased were farm fresh or free-range, all the meat and poultry products were farm-raised or organic and the fish were wild-caught? In my mind, the meals were healthy. So, I looked forward to gaining insight about causation and what to do next nutritionally at the upcoming appointment. Unfortunately, beyond running the standard tests, talking about how commonplace flutters were and

checking the boxes on what were clearly routine questions, the only other queries the doctor responded to were about watches! From dress and aviator to race and dive, Anthony and the cardiologist spent 30 minutes talking about watches and, beyond intimations about heredity, little to no time answering my questions about causation or nutrition.

Less than three months later, Anthony told me that he'd seen blood in his stool on and off for about a month and I immediately thought, cancer. While he was good at masking worry, years of family trauma surrounding the intersection of death and chronic disease stripped me of any ability to hide such things.

After convincing Anthony to schedule an emergency appointment with his physician for a referral to a gastroenterologist, I was filled with guilt for tip-toeing around in the plant-based lifestyle as opposed to taking the full plunge after being introduced to the documentary, "Forks Over Knives," a couple of weeks prior. Now deep-dive ready, I headed to the kitchen, dragged the trash can over to the fridge and dumped everything dairy, fish, meat, milk and eggs, never to be seen in my house again. While neither of Anthony's health scares ended up being chronic disease, I knew what kind of heartache was waiting if I didn't figure out how to make the knee-jerk reaction change, permanent.

My Vegucation

Next was my vegucation, which I believed to be the key to enduring change. To my delight, I discovered one of the featured doctors in the "Forks Over Knives" documentary, Dr. T. Colin Campbell partnered with Cornell University to create an online certification program for whole-food, plant-based nutrition, (eCornell, center for nutrition studies) and I registered the following week. That deep-dive into the benefits of whole-food, plant-based (WFPB) nutrition, the inherent health-degrading effects of the standard American diet, facts about federal agriculture guidelines, policies and subsidies and their harmful environmental impacts and the overwhelming volume of science-based evidence regarding food and nutrition changed my life.

With my 'why's' now secured and my seeds in full bloom, I fully incorporated my newfound vegucation into every facet of my life.

As a Coach and Culinary Entrepreneur, it was both a moral and an ethical imperative that my company, Herban-Eats, also fully adapt to the changes I made personally. Ready to leave a large segment of my target market behind, several colleagues, mentors, family and friends shunned me for the radical business change. From the cruelty of animal agriculture and its damaging environmental impact to sharing the science regarding the significant increased risk factors for chronic disease just by eating meat and dairy, they just couldn't understand why I was unwilling to just add vegan options and still profit from the sale of meat and dairy. Thankfully, I understood completely and moved forward just the same. Armed with my WFPB certification and a renewed company mission to *radicalize wellness with food*, I was ready to reshape my brand around a mission I could fully embrace.

From coaching, catering and vegucating, to live cooking demos, cooking classes and product lines, the more I learn, the more I pour into the business with the hope that sharing will have either an awakening or an affirming effect on family, friends, clients and community, and for many, it's done just that.

Tending the blooms of health curiosity and sharing the message that we never again have to normalize untimely disability and death, brought about by preventable, treatable and in many cases, reversible chronic diseases, continues to be one of the blossoms of my 'why.' Finding and embracing your 'why' is the key to lasting change. If you're struggling to identify a 'why,' I've included a few for you to consider within these pages.

Best wishes and continued success on your health-wealth journey!

Plant-Based, Vegan Culinarian and Vegucator

FLAVA NEWS YOU CAN USE

In an effort to clear the cluttered lanes of confusion that crowd almost every corner of the health news marketplace, these credible, peer-reviewed findings will help you better navigate your health-wealth journey with the kind of news you can use.

Chronic Disease

According to an empirical study published online March 1, 2018 (PMID 29494555) by the National Institute of Health (NIH), the Centers for Disease Control (CDC) found that 46% or 133 million Americans suffer from at least one chronic disease. The CDC also found that chronic disease accounts for 75% of aggregate healthcare spending or $5,300 per American family annually. With chronic disease accounting for 7 out of every 10 deaths (just under 2 million a year and rising), it's important to take a look at our top preventable, and in many cases, reversible chronic diseases so that we can get a handle on some real truths: 1. Our system of healthcare is severely broken 2. Moderation doesn't work 3. We can change our health-destiny with a few simple changes and choices.

Cardiovascular Vascular Disease (CVD)

According to the American Heart and Stroke Associations,CVD is the world and our nation's number 1 killer. 92 million Americans live with CVD and 837,000 Americans (1 in 3) die every year from it. On average, CVD costs $329.7 billion a year in the US, where nearly half of all African-Americans are living with some form of the disease.

According to the World Health Organization (WHO), 17.9 million people die every year from CVD, which accounts for about 31% of deaths worldwide.

Cancer

According to the National Cancer Institute and cancer.gov 1.7 million Americans will be diagnosed with cancer and over 605,000 will die from it; all within the span of one calendar year. On average, cancer costs $147.3 billion a year in the US, where the mortality is highest among African-Americans.

According to the WHO, there are 14.1 million new worldwide cases of cancer treated annually, of which 8.2 million will die of cancer-related deaths. By 2030 that number is expected to increase to 23.6 million new cases annually.

Benefits of a Whole-Food, Plant-Based (WFPB) or *Healthy* Vegan lifestyle

According to the National Academy of Sciences eating a WFPB lifestyle or otherwise *healthy* vegan diet could reduce mortality rates while also simultaneously reducing healthcare costs, greenhouse gas emissions and aiding greatly in the preservation of our very limited supply of freshwater. A 2019 major report released by the United Nations (UN) found that switching away from meat toward a plant-based diet is crucial to fighting climate change.

Mortality: Reduce your risk factors! Practicing a WFPB lifestyle, which includes but isn't limited to, food choices and 30 minutes a day of moderate exercise (brisk walking), can reduce your risk factors for chronic disease by up to 90%.

Healthcare: Save a Trillion! Including the cost of lost work days, healthcare in the US carries a price tag of $3.1 trillion a year (20% of gross domestic product). Practicing a WFPB or *healthy* vegan diet could translate into a $1 trillion dollar annual savings.

Saving Money: Bank up to $5k/year! Whether rolling your savings into your investment portfolio or taking that well-deserved vacation, practicing a WFPB lifestyle can lead to savings with your grocery budget of up to $5k a year! From big box stores and bag-it yourself grocers to local farm cooperatives and farmers' markets, whole grains, beans, legumes, fruits, veggies and nuts sold in bulk bins, bushels or cans are often well priced; saving you money at checkout. Local markets and cooperatives also tend to have the best tasting produce because they are picked at the height of freshness and sold immediately to you with no stops at processing centers or long hauls on trailers. Many begin their journey with meat alternatives and while that's fine to start, it's not a cost-savings or health-wealthy model. With the exception of a few mock meats touting a short list of recognizable ingredients, these products tend to be highly processed, and are sometimes as expensive and calorie-laden as the meat you're leaving behind. So, if keeping costs low matters, limit the mock meat alternative products to special events or occasions after you've made your transition into a plant-based or healthy vegan lifestyle.

Water: Saving it for them! Since it literally takes 1,000 gallons of water to produce one gallon of cow's milk, 55 gallons of water to produce two slices of dairy cheese and the equivalent of six months of showers for one person to produce one pound of meat, moving to a WFPB or *healthy* vegan diet can make a world of difference. In fact, according to People for the Ethical Treatment of Animals (PETA), when one person goes vegan, we save about 219,000 gallons of water a year, which will mean a lot more to your children and grandchildren.

Emissions: Decreasing your food emissions footprint! Practicing a WFPB or *healthy* vegan diet would reduce food-based emissions by a whopping 70%. Cutting food-based gas emissions also carries an annual savings value of $570 billion dollars.

Animal Welfare & Factory Farming: Growing up with a portion of meat at almost every meal, it's hard to paint a picture of empathy for the abused, sentient animals in society. We love our sentient pets but we normally don't equate the sentient animals we eat, aka 'the meat', with our pets because we normally aren't raising them, seeing them in the factory farms or slaughtering them. In fact, by the time we see them, they are neatly packaged or prominently displayed in stores so it's almost impossible to make a connection with them beyond anything but a food source. And while we know they are at least as intelligent and as sentient as our domestic pets, advertising, marketing, proximity to fast food and a lack of knowledge about how they are raised, treated and processed, tends to be an avoided topic. For these and other health-related reasons, this topic must be introduced here, at least in summary. It's a lot to take in so I'll limit the summary information to only one group, with the hope that it might encourage you to learn more through our resource list.

Chickens: 50 billion chickens a year are consumed worldwide; 9 billion a year in the U.S. 305 million egg laying hens a year are forced to overproduce and once spent, are slaughtered for pet food and chicken noodle soup. 200 million male chicks from egg laying hens are slowly starved and suffocated in large trash bins or ground alive in commercial grinding machines right after they are identified as male. 99% of farmed animals in the U.S. are factory-raised and spend the 6-7 weeks of their lives, prior to the ride to the slaughterhouse, in cramped, unsanitary, diseased facilities (approximately 30,000 crowded together in their own urine and fecal matter without the benefit of fresh air or sunlight). At the feed store, farmers without any veterinary prescriptions, purchase as much Prozac, arsenic, and other antibiotics as they desire. This cocktail is then well mixed and distributed into the feed or the water drip to increase size, spur faster growth and to keep them calm and alive in their inescapably nightmarish environment.

Whether it's your personal health, the advocacy of animals or the preservation of a healthy planet, changing the way you eat makes sense for a myriad of meaningful reasons.

Listed are a few websites, clinicians and scholars to dive into:
Websites: nutritionfacts.org , pcrm.org, peta.org
Clinicians to watch (Youtube): Milton Mills, MD, Baxter Montgomery, MD, Kim A. Williams Sr. MD, Michael Greger, MD, Dean Ornish, MD, Neal Barnard, MD, Caldwell Esselstyn, MD, John McDougall, MD, Garth Davis, MD, Michael Klaper, MD, Dr. T. Colin Campbell, Dr. Bobby J. Price, Brooke Goldner, MD, Sunil Pai, MD, Terry Mason, MD, Saray Stancic, MD, Michelle McMacken, MD, Dr. Pam Popper, ND, Dr. Cyrus Khambatta, Susan Levin RD, Dr. Ruby Lathon, Dr. Amie Breeze Harper, Tracye McQuirter, Russell Simmons.

PLANT-BASED & VEGAN LIFESTYLE FAQS

As a Whole-Food Plant-Based certified Vegan Nutrition Coach and Culinarian, I receive a lot of questions from people on their journey to health-wealth. Below, I've compiled the most common questions and best answers!

Q. Where can I go to find articles, peer-reviewed studies and data that supports the health benefits of a healthy vegan and/or WFPB lifestyle?
With thousands of these studies readily accessible, here are just a few: Nurses Health Studies, Adventist Studies, Interheart Study, Harvard Health Study & Harvard Health Follow Up Study, China/Oxford Study . Dean Ornish, MD Study, Caldwell Esselstyn MD Study, Framingham Heart Study, EPIC Study.

Q. Are there any differences between choosing a vegetarian, a vegan or whole-food, plant-based lifestyle as it relates to intake of fat and sugar?
According to a recent dietary composition study by JG Sobieski, there are significant distinctions between vegetarians, vegans, and a whole-food, plant-based (WFPB) lifestyle as it relates to total fat and sugar consumption compared to omnivores (meat eaters). Below is a chart indicating those variances:

	Omnivore	Vegetarian	Vegan	WFTB*
Total fat	830.9g	30g	30.4g	~10
Total sugar	22.9g	22.9g	22.6g	~10

*Approximate goal for WFPB with minimal or no added fat.

Vegetarians

Vegetarians exclude all meat and poultry from their diets but some eat eggs, seafood and dairy. While the #1 source of calcium in the U.S. is dairy (no matter the % or type) it's also the #1 source of artery-clogging saturated fats and one of the top allergens in the U.S. food supply.

Vegans

While the term "vegan" is now commonly used generally to identify people who refrain from eating meat and all other forms of animal products, vegan is a more broad term that has various subsets. Originally, the term vegan referred to those abstaining from the use of animal products, particularly in diet, and as an associated philosophy that rejects the commodity status of sentient beings. Many vegans also champion the cause of environmental protection. More a movement than a diet, vegan eating habits vary greatly. From the raw vegan to the junk food vegan, there are numerous animal-free diet places to land along the vegan spectrum. Because the term vegan is so widely used today, the only thing that's clear when you hear it is what's omitted from the plate; all animal products.

Whole-Food, Plant-Based (WFPB)

The WFPB lifestyle emphasizes minimally processed 'whole' foods and 30 minutes a day of moderate exercise (i.e., brisk walk). Food includes: an unlimited intake of minimally processed whole grains, fruits, veggies, legumes/beans, a limited intake of nuts, seeds, natural sweeteners and certain soy and tofu products not containing added fats. While the vast majority of WFPB devotees don't use ingredients or food that comes from animals, there are geographically specific pockets in the WFPB spectrum that do ingest minimal amounts of animal as food (see Blue Zones). However, I personally don't recommend or promote this incorporation.

Q. Is olive or coconut oil healthy?
There is little to no nutrient value in coconut, olive or any other oil. Any highly processed whole food, such as coconuts or olives, lose their nutritional value during the extraction and processing phases. A study (citation: Clin Cardiol. 1999 Jun; 22 (6 Suppl): II34-9. ncbi.nim.nih.gov) revealed significant flow mediated dilation (FMD) impairment, which measures flow mediated changes to the brachial artery, after the ingestion of high fat meals. Olive oil was found to have the same impairment to endothelial cells (which are cells all over the body that are involved in blood clotting and providing a barrier between the blood and the rest of our body tissues) as the rest of the high fat meals in the study. A more recent study (citation: Nutr Metab Cardiovascular Dis. 2007 Jan; 17(1): 50-7 ncbi.nim.nih.gov) showed similar effects on endothelial function after intake of palm, oil and soybean oils. If you have a chronic disease avoid oil at all costs. If you don't, understand; it's not health-promoting.

Q. Why are fruits & veggies so expensive?
One of the reasons is the allocation of spending through the US Department of Agriculture; farm subsidies program. According to a 2016 Metonomics study, the U.S. government subsidizes animal agriculture (meat, dairy and eggs) to the tune of $38 billion a year while only spending $17 million a year with fruit and vegetable agriculture. The government also subsidizes pro-meat and dairy advertising. So, if you're a tax-paying vegan, your taxes are also being allocated in support of animal agriculture and its promotion.

Q. I eat mostly skinless lean chicken, is that healthy?
1. Skinless chicken doesn't make chicken fat-free or healthy because much of the fat in chicken is in the muscle (meat) itself. Chickens have also been genetically manipulated through selective breeding; containing 2 to 3 times more calories from fat than from protein. In fact, a serving of chicken contains just as much cholesterol as red meat.
2. One of the largest cohort studies in the World European Prospective Investigation into Cancer and Nutrition, also know as the EPIC study, followed 477,000 people for 10 years, revealing that there was a 72% increased risk of pancreatic cancer for every 50 grams (just under 2 ounces) of chicken consumed daily. The EPIC study also referenced that the growth-promoting drugs fed to chickens and turkeys play a role but that there may also be cancer viruses in the poultry itself.

Q. Where will I get my protein?
The quick answer is, the same place the animals get it; plants. Made from the building blocks of 21 amino acids, 9 of the these amino acids, commonly referred to as the essential amino acids, must come from food. Interstingly, animals cannot create these essential amino acids, only plants do. Eating a variety of plant foods rich in amino acids is easy, affordable and will more than provide what the body needs to make the protein and related compounds it needs to thrive.

Q. How much protein do I need?
According to data published in the Journal of the American Medical Association (JAMA), diseases linked to unhealthful diets and lifestyle choices are the leading causes of death in the U.S. Because of the way protein is marketed, this is a common question but since people eating healthy vegan or plant-based diets aren't suffering from protein deficiencies, it's an unusual one. The best source of protein is the primary source, which is plants, not animals (remember, plants, not animals, make amino acids). The average person needs 50 to 70 grams of protein a day, which can be calculated using the following formula: your body weight x .36 grams = how much protein you should be consuming everyday. For example if you weigh 155 lbs just multiply 155 x .36 = 55.8 grams.

Q. Why hasn't my physician shared this information with me?
One would think that physicians would be fully equipped to render both pharmaceutical and nutrition-based protocols but, in most cases, you'd be wrong. Only 27% of U.S. medical schools offer a single course in nutrition and of those schools, medical students receive less than 20 hours of nutrition education over 4 years. For the other 73% of medical schools, their students receive no nutritional education whatsoever. So, beyond their personal lifestyle choices, it's unlikely that your physician knows or has taken the time to review any of the thousands of evidence-based, peer-reviewed trials, meta analysis, journals or articles related to nutrition, or more specifically, plant-based nutrition.

Plant Protein, Fiber & Cholesterol Table

1 cup serving	Quinoa	Tofu	Black beans	Oats	Sweet potatoes	Edamame	Chickpeas	Lentils	Farro
Protein	8g	20g	14g	6g	4g	9g	14.5g	18g	15g
Fiber	5.2g	2.6g	17g	4g	6.6g	8g	12g	16g	11g
Cholesterol	0	0	0	0	0	0	0	0	0

Table information sourced from nutritionix.com and healthline.com

RECIPES

$ $25 OR LESS $$ $26 OR MORE

"OUR GREATEST WHY" HE

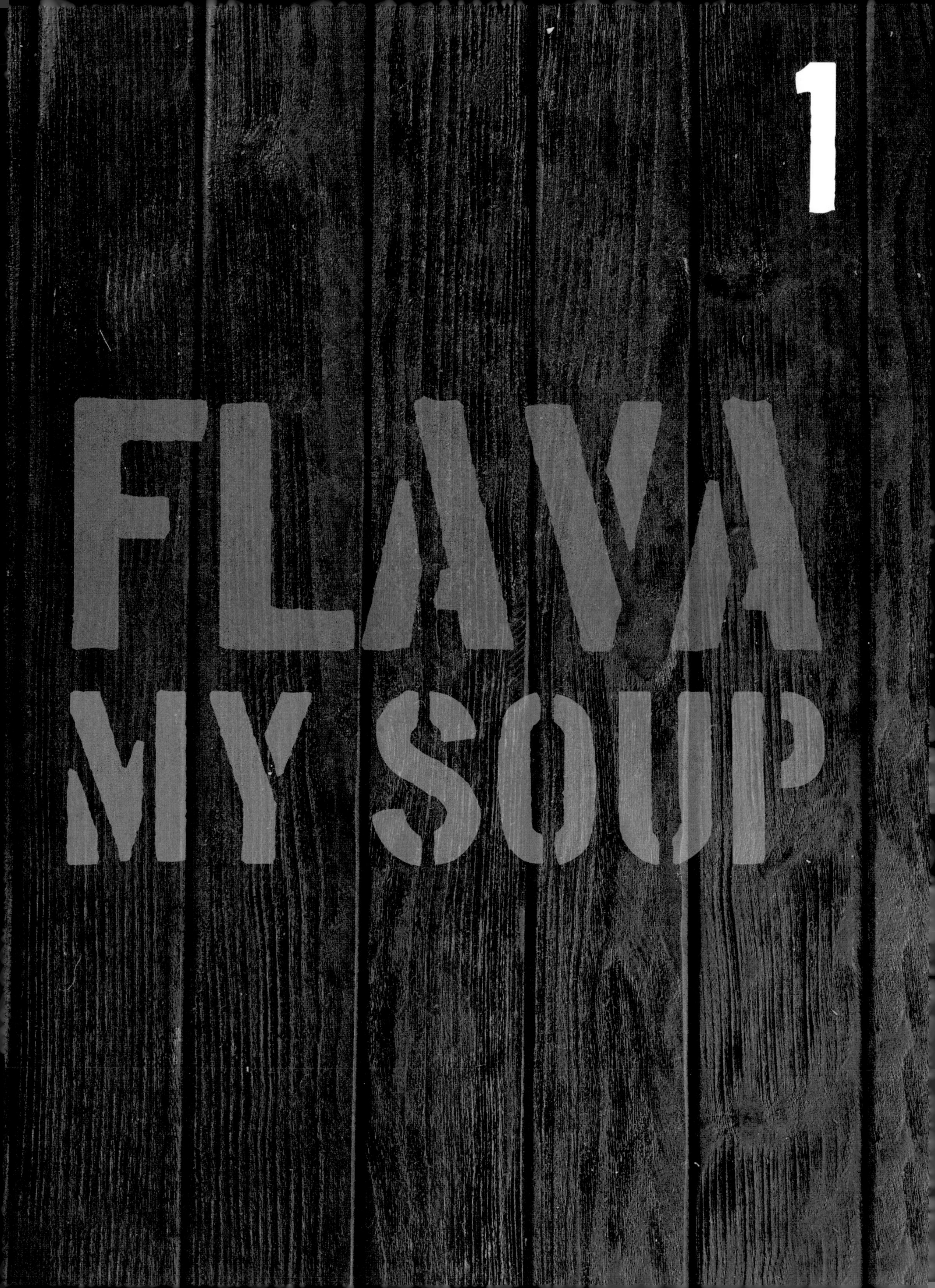
1
FLAVA
MY SOUP

LATIN BLACK BEAN & TOMATO STEW

35 MINS

With over 40,000 types of beans out there, one of the top three in the world are black beans. From side dishes and mains to desserts and appetizers, you are only limited by your imagination for ways to use this versatile, affordable bean. Brimming with protein, fiber and minerals, this flavor-packed quick and easy soup eats like a stew you took hours to prepare.

SERVES 6

- 3 – 15 oz cans of black beans, rinsed and drained
- ½ cup yellow onions, finely diced
- 2 cloves of garlic, minced
- 1 tsp grapeseed oil (or water)
- 1 – 15 oz can of fire roasted or regular diced tomatoes, undrained
- 1 tsp tomato paste
- ¼ cup cilantro, chopped
- 5 cups water
- ¼ tsp ground black pepper
- 2 tsp dried oregano
- ¼ tsp kosher salt (optional)
- 1 ¼ tsp ground cumin
- ¼ tsp ground coriander
- ½ tsp smoked paprika
- 1 tbsp raw cane sugar or organic agave nectar

Equipment: **dutch oven or large pot, serving bowl, knife, measuring spoon and cups, can opener, strainer/colander, mixing spoon**

1. Warm pot over medium heat, add oil, (3 tbsp of water if substituting) onions and cook about 5 minutes or until translucent.
2. Drop heat to medium–low, add tomato paste, garlic and all dry ingredients, with the exception of the sugar, and cook another 4 minutes, stirring consistently (so garlic won't burn and spices evenly distribute).
3. Increase temperature to medium high, add water, stir and bring to a low rolling boil.
4. Add diced tomatoes, sugar and stir for about 2 minutes then add black beans, stir to combine, drop temperature to low, cover with lid and cook for 20 minutes.
5. Once finished, remove from heat, check for consistency (may need more water; if so, add in ¼ cup increments) add cilantro and stir to combine.

TIP: If you're looking for a thicker stew, grab a potato masher and do a good mash in a corner of your pot then stir.

EASY OKRA & TOMATO STEW

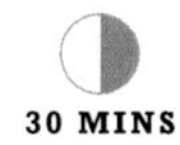

30 MINS

I didn't grow up enjoying okra but I did love tomatoes early on and thankfully, the southern part of my rearing introduced me to the classic tradition of okra and tomatoes! Common to most, if not all southern foodies, this is a summertime dish that, when cooked right, never fails to impress and bathe our organs with tons of health-promoting goodness. Here's our take on the classic!

SERVES 6

2 ½ cups okra, cleaned, cut in ¼ inch pieces
8 heirloom or vine grape tomatoes, quartered (makes 2 ½ cups)
1 cup yellow onions, diced
2 cloves of garlic, minced
2 tsp grapeseed oil (or water)
⅛ – ¼ cup water
¾ tsp ground black pepper
¼ tsp kosher salt (optional)

Equipment: large pan, dutch oven, serving bowl, knife, measuring spoon and cups

1. Place pan over medium heat. Add oil (or 3 tbsp water if substituting), onions and garlic and cook for 4 minutes or until onions become translucent.
2. Add tomatoes and their juices (from cutting board) to the pan, stir to combine, lower the temperature, cover with lid, drop temperature to low and allow the mixture to simmer gently for about 7 minutes.
3. Add the okra and ⅛ cup water, stir to combine, replace lid and cook for an additional 5 minutes.
4. Remove lid, add any additional water for preferred consistency, remove from heat. Serve and enjoy!

ROASTED BUTTERNUT SQUASH SOUP

50 MINS

Because of its wide flavor versatility, health benefits and ease of storage there's no time of year where soup isn't on the menu and while this soup is a warm, comforting one, it's satisfying year-round. Roasting the squash brings forward a much more rich and nutty taste and the addition of the pears and make this creamy, dreamy soup an easy choice.

SERVES 6

- 4 butternut squash, seeded and cubed (4 cups)
- ¾ cup shallots, peeled and diced
- 2 cloves of garlic, roasted or minced
- 1 tsp grapeseed oil (or water)
- ½ cup vegan cream cheese (optional)
- 1 cup Bartlett or Anjou pear, peeled and finely diced
- 1 cup low sodium vegetable stock
- 3 cups water
- ½ tsp ground black pepper
- ¾ tsp kosher salt (optional)
- ½ tsp ground coriander
- 2 tbsp fresh sage (or ½ tsp ground sage)
- Chives, chopped (for garnish)

Equipment: dutch oven or large pot, pan, serving bowl, knife, measuring spoon and cups, large baking sheet lined with parchment, immersion blender or high powered blender

1. Preheat oven to 400°F, prepare baking sheet with parchment and set aside.
2. Place cubed squash in mixing bowl, add ½ tsp salt, coriander, ¼ tsp black pepper and a teaspoon of oil (optional you can add 3 tablespoons of water or stock here) and toss to combine.
3. Distribute squash evenly on baking sheet and place on middle rack for 30 minutes (less time if your cubes are small and evenly cut) turn halfway through cooking then set aside.
4. Place pan over medium high heat, add oil (or 2 tbsp water, if substituting) pears, ¼ tsp pepper, ¼ tsp salt and sauté for 5 minutes (stirring occasionally). Add fresh sage last 3 minutes, remove from heat and set aside.
5. To your pan, add oil (or 2 tbsp water), shallots and sauté 4–5 minutes or until softened then set aside in bowl with pears.
6. If you have an immersion blender, place all ingredients (with the exception of the chives and vegan cream cheese) in your dutch oven/pot over medium heat and blend with your immersion blender to combine until smooth. If you are using a high powered blender, add all ingredients in small batches and puree until smooth and pour back into your dutch oven or pot (be careful when pouring warm product in your blender).
7. Once soup begins to low boil, turn heat to low, cover with lid and simmer for 15 minutes (stirring halfway through cooking).
8. Once finished, remove from heat, add cream cheese, stir, serve with garnish and enjoy!

LOADED VEGGIE SOUP

50 MINS

$

No matter the time of year, little feels more like home than a warm bowl of homemade vegetable soup. I remember fondly those days when I was too sick to go to school and my mommy would bring up a tray of vegetable soup, crackers and a big tablespoon. Recreating that kind of warmth in a recipe was important to include, not to mention delicious, freezable and healthy!

SERVES 8

- 3 medium yellow squash, cubed
- 2 medium zucchini, cubed
- 4 medium carrots, peeled and diced
- 4 large red potatoes, cubed
- 3 cups of baby kale or spinach, rinsed and rough chopped
- 2 – 15 oz cans of cannellini beans, rinsed
- 1 – 15 oz can of regular diced tomatoes (optional)
- 1 ½ cup leeks, washed and diced
- 3 cloves of garlic, minced
- ¾ tsp ground black pepper
- 1 tbsp dried oregano
- 2 bay leaves
- 6 sprigs fresh thyme
- 2 tbsp tamari or liquid aminos
- 1 tsp grapeseed oil (or 2 tsp water)
- 4 cups low sodium vegetable stock
- 4 cups water

Equipment: **dutch oven or large pot, knife, measuring spoon and cups, can opener, strainer/colander, potato masher, serving bowls**

1. Over medium heat, add oil (or 2 tbsp water, if substituting) leeks (or onions) and cook for 4 minutes or until translucent. Add garlic (if using water, add 2 more tbsp water) and cook another 2 minutes.
2. Add stock, water, tamari or aminos, potatoes, carrots, optional diced tomatoes, dried spices, bay leaves, fresh thyme, bring to a rolling boil, drop heat to low and cover with a lid. Allow to simmer 20 minutes.
3. Add the squash, zucchini and half of the beans. Mash the other half of the beans with a potato masher until well-mashed then add to the pot and stir to ensure it is well distributed (not clumped in one place). Replace lid and cook for 15 minutes.
4. Turn off the heat, remove the bay leaves and thyme stems, add kale (or spinach), stirring until it wilts. Check for seasoning and enjoy!

RECIPES

"OUR GREATEST WHY" HE

2
FLAVA
MY SALAD

LOADED FARRO SALAD

With over 40,000 varieties of cultivated rice, leaning toward whole grains was an easy decision. Packed with fiber, nutrients and antioxidants, whole grains and ancient grains are health-wealth champions. Originating in the fertile crescent and found in the tomb of Egyptian Pharaohs, farro is a nutrient-dense, emmer or einkorn wheat variety grain that packs twice the protein punch of brown rice and will satisfy even the most picky eaters!

SERVES 8

- 4 cups of cooked farro (cook per package directions)
- 1–12 oz package or ¾ cup meatless crumbles (optional)
- 1 cup sun dried tomatoes, julienned (no oil)
- 1 cup cleaned, chopped leeks
- ¼ cup Italian flat leaf parsley, chopped
- ¾ tsp smoked paprika
- ¾ tsp garlic powder
- ½ tsp black or white pepper
- ½ tsp kosher salt (optional)
- 2 tbsp olive oil (or water)

Equipment: **Large pan, baking sheet with parchment paper or silpat, spatula/spoon, knife, medium to large serving bowl, measuring cup, measuring spoons, medium sized pan, small mixing bowl**

1. Preheat oven to 400°F and prepare your baking pan with parchment paper or silpat.
2. Place prepared leeks in a bowl and season with ½ tsp olive oil (or 1 tbsp water if substituting), ¼ tsp smoked paprika, ½ tsp garlic powder and ¼ tsp black pepper, toss to evenly distribute spices and spread evenly across the baking pan and place on middle rack for 10 minutes then remove and set aside.
3. Place your nonstick pan over medium–high heat and add a teaspoon of olive oil (or 2 tbsp water if substituting) then crumble in your crumbles. Break the mixture apart with your spatula or wooden spoon and cook for about 3 minutes.
4. Add the remaining garlic powder, salt, smoked paprika and pepper to the crumbles pan, stir and continue cooking for another 3 minutes to render a crispier and browner appearance to the crumbles.
5. Add the sun-dried tomatoes and combine well with your crumbles. Make sure the tomaotes are getting some direct heat from the pan (if the pan is dry you may want to add a tbsp of water) cook about 3 minutes then set aside.
6. In your large serving bowl with the farro, add leeks, parsley, sun dried tomatoes and crumble mix and toss and fold to incorporate. Add your fresh herbs, an optional 1 tsp of olive oil then re-toss and serve.

NORTH / SOUTH BUDDHA BOWL

35 MINS

For me, almost any buddha bowl is a winner because it's built around a powerhouse of plant-power: grains, protein, nuts/seeds and veggies. This southern buddha bowl is a nod to my northern roots and my southern upbringing, which is the best of any food world!

SERVES 4

- 3 large sweet potatoes cut into ½ inch or small cubes
- 1 cup chickpeas (garbanzo beans), rinsed and drained
- 1 cup black eyed peas, rinsed and drained
- 1 ½ cups cooked farro
- 3 cups purple cabbage, cored, quartered and chopped
- 2 cups shredded carrots
- 1 cup red or yellow peppers, seeded and diced
- ½ cup chives
- ¼ cup flat leaf parsley
- 1 cup pecans, chopped
- ¾ tsp ground black pepper
- ½ tsp kosher salt
- ¾ tsp cumin
- 1 tsp paprika
- 1 tsp garlic powder
- ½ tsp coriander

FOR THE DRESSING

- 2 tbsp harissa
- 2 tsp agave nectar or maple syrup
- 3 tbsp coconut aminos or tamari
- 2 tsp unseasoned rice vinegar
- ½ tsp lime juice
- ¾ to 1 cup grapeseed oil (opt for veg stock if you're oil free)

Equipment: **mixing bowls, knife, measuring spoon and cups, 2 baking sheets, parchment paper or silpat, aluminum foil, spatulas, 4 serving bowls and cooking gloves**

1. Preheat oven to 400°F and prepare your 2 nonstick or lined baking sheets then set aside.
2. In a mixing bowl, add sweet potatoes, 1 tsp olive oil (or 2 tsp of water if substituting), and ½ of all your dried spices then stir to combine. Evenly distribute potatoes on baking sheet and place in oven on middle rack for 30 minutes (be sure to turn every 10 minutes so they don't burn). Remove from oven, cover with aluminum foil and set aside.
3. In a mixing bowl add your black-eyed peas and garbanzos (chickpeas) and season with other half of your dried spices, 1 tsp oil (or 2 tsp water if substituting) and combine. Evenly distribute black eyed peas and chickpea mixture on baking sheet. Bake for 10 minutes then remove from oven, place in a bowl and set aside.
4. In the bottom of a mixing bowl add your dressing ingredients, whisk until combined, remove half of the dressing and combine with your peas and beans mixture. Add the remaining half and pour it over your, cabbage and carrot mixture and massage with your gloved hands to break down the cabbage and to integrate the dressing flavor into the cabbage. Place cabbage mixture in fridge for about 10 minutes.
5. Remove cabbage and carrot mixture from fridge, pull out your 4 serving bowls, then set up your roasted sweet potatoes, cooked farro, peas and beans mixture and cabbage carrot mixture for easy assembly.
6. In bottom of the individual bowls, place your cabbage and carrot mixture then creatively place remaining items beside each other in the bowl or atop one another (be creative), then enjoy!

SPICY SWEET POTATO SALAD

35 MINS

$

Whether served on a bed of kale or as a complement to a main dish, this nutty, soft-spiced sweet salad is great to serve year-round. The sweet of the roasted potato and the gentleness of the spices makes this salad a crowd-pleaser.

SERVES 6

- 5 sweet potatoes, peeled and cut into ½ inch cubes
- ¼ cup red onion, finely diced
- ½ cup dried cranberries, soaked in ⅔ cup of warm water (20 mins), drained and rough chopped
- 5 tbsp grapeseed oil
- 1 cup shelled pistachios, rough chopped (optional)
- ½ tsp orange zest
- 2 tbsp juice from freshly squeezed orange
- ½ tsp lemon zest
- ½ cup flat leaf parsley, chopped
- ¼ tsp ground black pepper
- ½ tsp kosher salt
- ¼ cup garlic powder
- ¾ tsp cumin
- ½ tsp coriander
- 1 tsp smoked paprika
- ¼ tsp ground ginger
- a pinch of allspice
- a pinch of cinnamon

Equipment: serving bowl, mixing bowl, knife, measuring spoon and cups, baking sheet, parchment paper or silpat

1. Preheat oven to 400°F and prepare nonstick or lined baking sheet then set aside.
2. In your mixing bowl add the sweet potatoes, 1 tbsp of oil (or 2 tbsp of water, if substituting), ½ tsp of smoked paprika, ¼ tsp garlic powder, ¼ tsp ginger and ¼ tsp salt, toss to evenly distribute then pour onto the baking sheet and place on middle rack for 30 minutes (turn the potatoes every 10 minutes so they don't burn) then remove from oven, cover with foil and set aside.
3. To the bottom of your mixing bowl, add remaining spices, orange zest, lemon zest and orange juice, and slowly whisk in ¼ cup of oil until combined.
4. Add your potatoes and the diced cranberries, fold into the dressing and set aside 5 minutes.
5. Add your chopped pistachios, red onions and fresh herbs and give it one more toss before serving and enjoy!

TIP: Unless you are ready to eat/serve this salad, don't dress it because the acid in the citrus will break down your salad. So, if you're making this ahead just prepare the dressing and place it in a small container and dress your salad a few minutes before eating.

EDAMAME SALAD

15 MINS

Whether steamed in the pod or shelled, there is something cool, refreshing and filling about Edamame. Healthful and versatile, I like to bring it to life by adding simple ingredients that enhance the flavor and nutrient-density of the dish while keeping them begging for seconds!

SERVES 6

- 5 – 12-oz frozen packs of shelled edamame (properly thawed)
- ¼ cup red onion, finely diced
- 1 ½ tbsp white wine vinegar
- 4 tbsp extra virgin olive oil
- ¼ tsp ground black pepper
- ¼ cup Italian flat leaf parsley, chopped
- ¾ cup pitted and rinsed kalamata olives, finely chopped or pulsed lightly in food processor

Equipment: serving bowl, mixing bowl, knife, measuring spoon and cups

1. Thaw your shelled edamame in your fridge, rinse in your colander and set aside.
2. In a large bowl or tightly lidded jar, whisk together or vigorously shake, vinegar, oil and pepper until well combined.
3. In a large bowl, add all your ingredients (except dressing) and mix well.
4. Fold in your dressing to integrate, place in the fridge about 15 minutes, then serve and enjoy!

TIP: If you aren't serving the whole salad or are meal prepping, do not dress the whole salad because the acidity of the vinegar will break down your edamame and take away from the dish. For meal prepping, place your dressing mix in a small airtight container and take it with you. This way you can dress your salad a few minutes before you eat.

GREENS & HEMPSEED PESTO PASTA SALAD

20 MINS

Looking for a salad that's loaded with protein, vitamins and nutrients but doesn't require you to eat a wagon full of greens? This recipe is it; ¼ cup of hempseed has a whopping 12 grams of protein 28mg of calcium, 480 mg of potassium and more! Commonly confused with, cannabis, hemp contains only trace amounts of THC and is more than safe to eat. Along for the pesto party is spinach, kale, basil, garlic and a little lemon juice to round things out. This is an easy, healthful and flavorful pasta salad or main dish and a go-to recipe when I'm introducing someone to vegan food because who doesn't love a good pesto!

SERVES 6

- 4 cups 100% whole grain pasta, cooked (I use penne rigate or shells)
- ¾ cup hemp seeds
- 1 ½ cups spinach, rough chopped
- 1 ½ cups kale, rough chopped (I like Lacinato or dino kale but curly is fine)
- ¼ cup basil, rough chopped
- 3 tbsp lemon juice
- zest of 1 lemon
- ½ tsp kosher salt (optional)
- 2–3 garlic cloves, minced
- ½ cup grapeseed oil (or water)

Equipment: food processor, knife, serving bowl, large mixing bowl, measuring cups and spoons, microplane or zester

1. Place your cooked pasta in a large mixing bowl and set aside.
2. Put the garlic and hempseed in your food processer and give it 3 to 4 quick pulses (about 5 seconds a pulse).
3. Add the spinach and basil and give it a couple of quick pulses, scrape down the sides, add the kale and give it a few pulses, then scrape down the sides again.
4. With the processor on low-speed, pour in the lemon juice, salt, pepper and oil (or ⅓ cup water, if substituting) then let it run until your pesto is smooth and creamy.
5. Check for flavor and texture. Like a regular pesto, it needs to be thinner than a paste but not runny like a dressing.
6. Pour over your pasta, being sure to scrape down the sides of the food processor bowl to get every little drop of this tasty sauce. Mix well to coat every noodle!

SALAD DRESSINGS

In an effort to save you money and frustration reading labels in the grocery store, I've put together some easy dressing recipes that require only a whisk or a high-powered blender. These will keep in your fridge just like any other dressing and are free of those pesky refined sugars, preservatives and additives.

BALSAMIC AND HERB DRESSING

MAKES 1¼ CUPS

¾ cup balsamic vinegar
2 tbsp Dijon mustard
1 tbsp lemon juice
¼ tsp agave
1 tbsp flat leaf parsley-chopped
¼ cup light olive or grapeseed oil or water
¼ tsp salt
black pepper to taste

Combine all of the ingredients (including the water if you're using it instead of oil) and blend or whisk, while slowly streaming in the oil. Taste for flavor then enjoy!

AGAVE DIJON DRESSING

MAKES 1¼ CUPS

¼ cup Dijon mustard
¼ cup lemon juice
1 ½ tbsp agave nectar
¾ tsp salt
½ tsp white or black ground pepper
¾ cup water or ⅔ cup grapeseed oil

Combine all of the ingredients (including the water if you're using it instead of oil) and blend or whisk, while slowly streaming in the oil. Taste for flavor then enjoy!

YUMMY RANCH DRESSING

MAKES 2 CUPS

1 cup raw cashews (if nut allergy substitute pumpkin seeds here)
1 tbsp lemon juice
zest of ½ lemon
1 tsp agave nectar
1 tsp stone ground or dijon mustard
¾ cup soy or preferred non-dairy milk
2 tsp unfiltered apple cider vinegar
½ cup light olive or grapeseed oil or water
1 tsp garlic powder
½ tsp coriander, ground
¾ tsp onion powder
½ tsp salt
¼ tsp white or black pepper
3 tbsp fresh dill

Combine all of the ingredients (including the water if you're using it instead of oil) and blend, while slowly streaming in the oil. Taste for flavor then enjoy!

PROTEIN PACKED ITALIAN DRESSING

MAKES 2 CUPS

¾ cup cannellini beans (drained and rinsed)
¾ cup water
2 tbsp lemon juice
¼ cup sundried tomatoes
2 cloves garlic, roasted
1 shallot, chopped
1 ½ tsp dried oregano
1 tsp agave nectar
¼ teaspoon salt
2 tbsp flat leaf parsley-chopped
½ tsp salt
¼ tsp white or black pepper

Combine all of the ingredients in a blender and pulse on low until rustic or completely smooth.

CHICKPEA NOT SO TUNA SALAD

20 MINS

$ $

A good tuna salad was worth its weight in gold as a yummy, easy, pack and go lunch option and this chickpea variation is even better! Packed with high protein, fiber and nutrients, you don't miss the flavors of the tuna salad because we bring it all to the ingredients (with the exception of the tuna) to the party!

SERVES 8

- 4 cups of spinach or your favorite salad green, rough chopped
- 1 cup cucumbers, chopped
- 1 cup cherry or grape tomatoes, halved
- 4 – 15 oz cans of chickpeas (also called garbanzos), rinsed and drained
- ¾ cup celery, finely chopped
- ½ cup red onions, finely chopped
- 3 tbsp fresh dill, chopped
- ⅔ cup vegan mayonnaise
- 1 ½ tbsp stone ground mustard
- zest of 1 lemon (1 tbsp)
- 1 tbsp dulse granules (or nori flakes, ground)
- ½ tsp garlic powder
- ¼ tsp black pepper
- ½ tsp kosher salt (optional)

Equipment: food processor, knife, large mixing bowl, serving bowl, measuring cups and spoons, microplane or zester

1. Combine the spinach, cucumbers, tomatoes and set aside in fridge.
2. In two cup batches, add your garbanzo or chickpeas to your food processer then quick pulse them 4 to 6 times to break them up (not to make them mush or paste, just so they're no longer whole), remove from processer, add to large mixing bowl and repeat until finished.
3. Add all remaining ingredients to the bowl and fold to combine.
4. Garnish with any extra dill and serve. If preparing ahead, place in fridge then add the dill and lemon zest combo just before serving and enjoy over your bed of greens with tomatoes, cucumbers and one of our dressings!

RECIPES

$ $25 OR LESS $$ $26 OR MORE

"OUR GREATEST WHY" HE

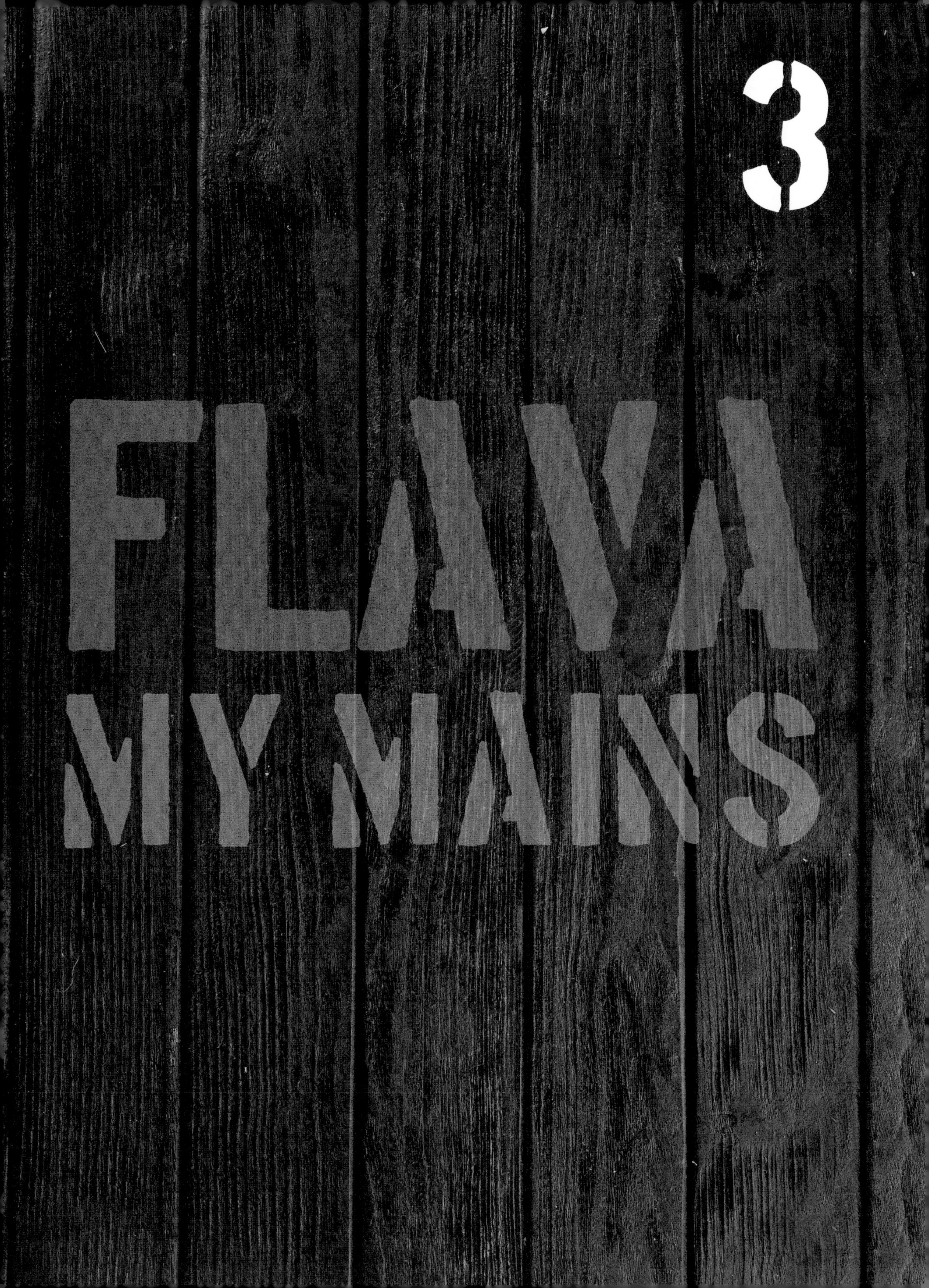
3
FLAVA
MY MAINS

LOADED LASAGNA

90 MINS

Whenever I think of Lasagna, I think of a comforting plate of firm-textured, creamy, saucy goodness with layers of pasta and I didn't want to lose that just because I stopped eating meat and dairy. So, here's the perfect recipe for those hankering for something familiar and absolutely delectable!

SERVES 8

14–16 sheets of whole grain lasagna, cooked (according to box directions)

FOR THE TOMATO SAUCE

2 – 10 oz packs sliced Baby Bella or white mushrooms, chopped (optional)
3 tbsp tamari lite (or soy sauce)
1 – 28 oz can crushed tomatoes
1 – 15 oz can fire-roasted diced tomatoes (drained)
¾ cup tomato paste
1 tbsp dried oregano
3 cloves garlic, minced
¾ tsp kosher salt (or to taste)
½ tsp black or white pepper or to taste
1 tsp cornstarch (if needed for thickening)

FOR THE MEATLESS CRUMBLES

3 – 12 oz packs of meatless crumbles
1 ½ cup yellow onion, finely diced
1 tsp grapeseed oil
½ tsp garlic powder (optional)
1 tsp oregano
½ tsp ground black pepper
2 – 9 oz bags of spinach, roughly chopped

FOR THE BECHAMEL (WHITE SAUCE)

½ cup + 2 tbsp grapeseed or canola oil
1 cup, all purpose unbleached flour, sifted
5 cups unsweetened, unflavored soy or almond milk
⅔ cup nutritional yeast
2 tbsp dijon mustard
1 tsp garlic powder
¾ tsp white pepper
½ tsp kosher salt
½ tsp onion powder

FOR THE TOPPING

5 vine-ripe or Roma tomatoes, thinly sliced
2 cups shredded Vegan Mozzarella
Course Ground Black Pepper

Equipment: **large mixing bowl, square or oblong casserole dish, large baking sheet, dutch oven or large pot, large pan with lid, whisk, wooden spoon, measuring cups and measuring spoons, colander, kitchen towel, bowls**

1. Preheat oven to 400°F and prepare casserole with a little oil to cover surface of dish.
2. Place dutch oven or large pot over medium heat and add 1 tsp of oil (or 2 tsps of water, if substituting). Add the mushrooms, tamari, combine and stir. Drop heat to low, cover with lid and cook for 7 minutes.
3. Remove lid, stir and continue to cook another 5 minutes, stirring regularly, to cook off excess water in pot and to brown mushrooms, then remove from pot and set aside.
4. Increase heat for dutch oven to medium low and add tomato paste, fresh garlic, pepper and salt to bottom of seasoned (or uncleaned mushroom dutch oven/pot). Stir and cook for about 4 minutes (to cook the raw flavor out of the tomato paste).
5. Reduce heat to low and add crushed tomatoes and fire roasted tomatoes to pot, stirring frequently for about 10 minutes. Return mushrooms to the pot, stir, move to a large bowl and set aside to cool in fridge for 20 minutes.
6. For the meatless crumbles, place a large nonstick pan over a medium heat and add 1 tsp of oil (or 1 tbsp water, if substituting), onions and cook for 5 minutes or until translucent then set aside in a bowl.
7. In the pan used to cook the onions, add the crumbles over medium heat, breaking up crumbles with spatula or spoon. Add garlic powder, oregano and pepper to crumbles and cook about 7 minutes then remove from heat and set aside in bowl with onions.
8. To the pan, add spinach, 1 tbsp of water and cook to wilt down over medium heat for 5 minutes, stirring occasionally. Once wilted down, place in kitchen towel or colander, to remove excess liquid, then combine to bowl with crumbles.
9. For the bechamel, place large pot over medium-low heat and add grapeseed oil and flour, whisking for about 3 minutes. Whisk in garlic powder, onion powder, pepper and salt and pour in one cup of plant milk at a time. Whisk continuously until sauce thickens (about 8 minutes – sauce also thickens off heat). Remove from heat, whisk in nutritional yeast, dijon mustard then set aside to cool in fridge 15 minutes.
10. For assembly: Base Layer: tomato sauce, next-pasta, next-tomato sauce, next-crumble mixture, next-bechamel, next-pasta and repeat leaving about ½ inch to top of casserole (about 3–4 layers). Finishing Layer: pasta then bechamel. Top with mozzarella, arrange the sliced tomatoes in rows, sprinkle with black pepper, bake uncovered on a large lined baking sheet for 45 minutes. Allow to cool 25 minutes before cutting.

SOUTHERN MAC & PLEASE

50 MINS

For many, the idea of passing over a creamy mac & cheese dish on holidays or any given soulful Sunday is almost sacrilegious. Passing over the meats is one thing but the idea of passing over your auntie's prized mac & cheese could get you kicked out of the house without a suitable substitute. With this in mind, we set out to make a soulful vegan mac & please that's so good you'd be comfortable placing alongside your auntie's for everyone to enjoy!

SERVES 6

- 6 cups whole wheat elbow macaroni or shells, cooked
- 1 – 8 oz vegan cream cheese
- ¼ cup vegan plant butter, softened (optional)
- ¾ cup shredded vegan cheddar or mozzarella
- ½ cup flat leaf parsley, chopped

FOR THE CRUMB TOPPING MIX

- 1 ½ cup panko or whole wheat bread crumbs
- ½ cup shredded vegan cheese (optional)
- 2 tbsp flat leaf parsley, finely chopped
- ½ tsp paprika
- ½ tsp pepper
- ¼ cup melted plant butter or grapeseed oil (or ¼ cup water)

FOR THE CHEESE SAUCE

- ¾ cup nutritional yeast
- 6 cups soy or other plant milk
- 1 cup soaked cashews, drained (Quick Soak Method)
- ⅔ cup carrots, peeled and diced
- ½ cup red potato, peeled and diced
- 1 tsp fresh lemon juice
- 1 tsp kosher salt
- 1 tbsp turmeric
- 1 tsp smoked paprika
- 1 tsp garlic powder
- ¾ tsp white or black pepper
- 2 ½ tbsp ground flaxseed

Equipment: one 13 – 9 inch casserole dishes or one large, deep casserole pan, measuring spoons and cups, large mixing bowl, high-powered blender, medium pot, spoons and spatulas, knife, smaller bowls, large baking pan with parchment paper (to set casserole dish on while baking) , aluminum foil

1. Preheat oven to 400°F.
2. Prepare pasta accordingly, set aside in large mixing bowl and while pasta is still warm, add vegan cream cheese, vegan butter, ¾ cup vegan cheddar or mozzarella and flat leaf parsley. Stir to combine and set aside.
3. Add carrots and potatoes to a pot filled with water ½ inch over mixture and bring to boil. Cook until tender (about 15–20 mins) then set aside.
4. Add all cheese sauce ingredients, including cooked carrots and potatoes to your blender, puree until completely smooth, then taste for flavor. This should be saucy, slightly soupy in texture.
5. Pour cheese sauce into your pasta bowl and stir to combine.
   Note: Much like regular mac and cheese, the consistency should be saucy; almost soupy. This is important because when the casserole goes in the oven it will firm up a bit so it shouldn't go into the oven already firm; it should be loose. Add more plant milk, if needed and stir to combine.
6. Pour into the casserole, cover with aluminum foil, place casserole on lined baking pan and bake for 20 minutes. While baking, combine all your crumb topping ingredients and set aside.
7. Remove from oven, sprinkle on your topping and return to the oven uncovered for 10 more minutes.
8. Remove from oven, allow to cool at least 15 minutes, then serve and enjoy!

Cashews: Quick Soak Method

Microwave: Place 1 cup of cashews in 1½ cups of water and microwave for 60 seconds then set aside for 20 minutes before use.

Stovetop: Add 1 cup of cashews to 1½ cups of water bring to a rolling boil then remove from heat, and place a tight fitting lid over it for 15 minutes.

PENNE A LA VODKA

30 MINS

On most Italian restaurant menus you'll find this popular dish and as a plant-based vegan you can still enjoy it. Surprise that special someone on date night or just treat yourself or your family (no worries, the alcohol cooks off) to this tasty dish alongside one of our salads.

SERVES 6

- 1 box of your favorite 100% whole wheat or gluten free penne pasta, cooked
- ¾ cup good vodka
- 1 – 28 oz can diced tomatoes
- ¾ cup tomato paste
- ¾ cup water
- 3 cloves of roasted or minced garlic
- ½ cup red bell peppers, diced
- ¾ cup yellow onion, finely chopped
- 1 tbsp grapeseed oil (or water)
- 1 tsp balsamic vinegar
- ¼ tsp Kosher salt
- ½ tsp white or black pepper
- 1 tbsp nutritional yeast
- ¾ cup raw cashews (place in bowl with about ½ inch of water covering them and microwave 60 seconds)
- ½ cup fresh basil, torn
- 2 tbsp flat leaf parsley, chopped

Equipment: **serving bowl, dutch oven or large pot, wooden spoon/spatula, knife, measuring cup, measuring spoon, blender and whisk (optional)**

1. Add oil (or 3 tbsp of water if substituting) onions, salt and pepper to your pot, stir and cook over medium heat about 5 minutes or until translucent.
2. Add red peppers and garlic and cook, stirring frequently (to avoid garlic burning) for another 3 minutes.
3. Add tomato paste and cook, stirring frequently, for 3 minutes then add water, diced tomatoes, balsamic vinegar and vodka. Stir, reduce to low and cook 20 minutes uncovered, stirring frequently.
4. While the sauce is cooking, add the undrained cashews and the nutritional yeast to your high powered blender and blend on puree or high until it is completely smooth and creamy (no lumps) then set aside.
5. Scrape all your cashew sauce into your sauce pot, stir and cook another 5 minutes then taste, add any additional seasoning, toss into your large serving bowl with your pasta, top with basil and parsley and enjoy!

ROASTED SWEET POTATO & SOY CHORIZO CHILI

60 MINS

Whether you like it with beans or without, who doesn't love a warm comforting bowl of chili? Since I enjoy playing with savory and sweet and including as many healthy additions as possible, the roasted sweet potato makes this recipe a home run with everyone who tries it!

SERVES 6

- 2 medium sized, roasted sweet potatoes
- 1 – 15 oz can of fire roasted or diced tomatoes, undrained
- 1-1 ½ packages (12 oz) soy chorizo
- 2 – 15 oz cans, dark red kidney beans, rinsed and drained
- 2 – 15 oz cans, cannelini beans, rinsed and drained
- 1 tsp grapeseed oil (or water)
- ½ cup yellow onion, finely diced
- ½ cup large red bell pepper, diced
- 3 cloves of garlic, minced
- ¼ cup tomato paste
- 1 tbsp agave nectar
- 2 ½ cups of water
- 3 tbsp chili powder
- ¾ tsp smoked paprika
- 2 tsp ground cumin
- 2 tsp dried oregano
- ¾ tsp kosher salt (optional)
- 1 cinnamon stick
- ¼ cup freshly chopped cilantro
- ¾ cup green onions diced (garnish)
- ½ tsp salt (optional)

Equipment: **dutch oven or large pot, can opener, colander (strainer), knife, measuring spoons, measuring cups, wooden spoon or spatula, baking pan/sheet, parchment paper, nonstick pan**

1. Preheat oven to 425°F and prepare baking sheet for potatoes and set aside.
2. Cut sweet potatoes in half lengthwise and rub all over, very lightly with oil, then place, cut side down, on parchment or silpat and put in middle rack of oven for 30 minutes (halfway through cooking, turn potatoes over) then remove from oven, cover with aluminum foil and set aside.
3. Once potatoes have cooled, you can cut vertically and horizontally (like a tic tac toe board) inside the potato halves then scoop them out (the pieces should be bite sized) and set aside.
4. Place a nonstick pan over medium–high heat and add a tsp of oil (or add 1 tbsp water, if substituting).
5. Remove casing from soy chorizo, add to pan and break it up with wooden spoon and cook, stirring regularly, for about 5 minutes then remove from heat and set aside.
6. Place dutch oven or large pot over medium heat and add chili powder, cumin, garlic powder and smoked paprika (stirring frequently) to toast for about one minute or until fragrant, then remove from heat and set aside in a bowl.
7. Place dutch oven or large pot over medium heat with 1 tsp of oil (or 1 tbsp water, if substituting) and add your onions; cooking 5 minutes or until translucent. Add red peppers and garlic, stir and combine with onions and cook 4 minutes.
8. Add tomato paste and toasted spices, stir to combine and cook, stirring regularly, for about 4 minutes (to cook the raw flavor out of the tomato paste). Add diced tomatoes, salt, agave, water, cinnamon stick, stir to combine. Bring to a rolling boil then drop temperature to low, and simmer with tightly fitted lid for 15 minutes.
9. Add beans, soy chorizo and sweet potatoes, gently stir to combine and simmer without lid, stirring regularly, for 10–15 minutes. Remove from heat, add cilantro, garnish with green onions and enjoy!

SOUTHERN MAC & PLEASE

50 MINS

For many, the idea of passing over a creamy mac & cheese dish on holidays or any given soulful Sunday is almost sacrilegious. Passing over the meats is one thing but the idea of passing over your auntie's prized mac & cheese could get you kicked out of the house without a suitable substitute. With this in mind, we set out to make a soulful vegan mac & please that's so good you'd be comfortable placing alongside your auntie's for everyone to enjoy!

SERVES 6

- 6 cups whole wheat elbow macaroni or shells, cooked
- 1 – 8 oz vegan cream cheese
- ¼ cup vegan plant butter, softened (optional)
- ¾ cup shredded vegan cheddar or mozzarella
- ½ cup flat leaf parsley, chopped

FOR THE CRUMB TOPPING MIX

- 1 ½ cup panko or whole wheat bread crumbs
- ½ cup shredded vegan cheese (optional)
- 2 tbsp flat leaf parsley, finely chopped
- ½ tsp paprika
- ½ tsp pepper
- ¼ cup melted plant butter or grapeseed oil (or ¼ cup water)

FOR THE CHEESE SAUCE

- ¾ cup nutritional yeast
- 6 cups soy or other plant milk
- 1 cup soaked cashews, drained (Quick Soak Method)
- ⅔ cup carrots, peeled and diced
- ½ cup red potato, peeled and diced
- 1 tsp fresh lemon juice
- 1 tsp kosher salt
- 1 tbsp turmeric
- 1 tsp smoked paprika
- 1 tsp garlic powder
- ¾ tsp white or black pepper
- 2 ½ tbsp ground flaxseed

Equipment: one 13 – 9 inch casserole dishes or one large, deep casserole pan, measuring spoons and cups, large mixing bowl, high-powered blender, medium pot, spoons and spatulas, knife, smaller bowls, large baking pan with parchment paper (to set casserole dish on while baking) , aluminum foil

1. Preheat oven to 400°F.
2. Prepare pasta accordingly, set aside in large mixing bowl and while pasta is still warm, add vegan cream cheese, vegan butter, ¾ cup vegan cheddar or mozzarella and flat leaf parsley. Stir to combine and set aside.
3. Add carrots and potatoes to a pot filled with water ½ inch over mixture and bring to boil. Cook until tender (about 15–20 mins) then set aside.
4. Add all cheese sauce ingredients, including cooked carrots and potatoes to your blender, puree until completely smooth, then taste for flavor. This should be saucy, slightly soupy in texture.
5. Pour cheese sauce into your pasta bowl and stir to combine.
   Note: Much like regular mac and cheese, the consistency should be saucy; almost soupy. This is important because when the casserole goes in the oven it will firm up a bit so it shouldn't go into the oven already firm; it should be loose. Add more plant milk, if needed and stir to combine.
6. Pour into the casserole, cover with aluminum foil, place casserole on lined baking pan and bake for 20 minutes. While baking, combine all your crumb topping ingredients and set aside.
7. Remove from oven, sprinkle on your topping and return to the oven uncovered for 10 more minutes.
8. Remove from oven, allow to cool at least 15 minutes, then serve and enjoy!

Cashews: Quick Soak Method

Microwave: Place 1 cup of cashews in 1½ cups of water and microwave for 60 seconds then set aside for 20 minutes before use.

Stovetop: Add 1 cup of cashews to 1½ cups of water bring to a rolling boil then remove from heat, and place a tight fitting lid over it for 15 minutes.

PENNE A LA VODKA

30 MINS

On most Italian restaurant menus you'll find this popular dish and as a plant-based vegan you can still enjoy it. Surprise that special someone on date night or just treat yourself or your family (no worries, the alcohol cooks off) to this tasty dish alongside one of our salads.

SERVES 6

- 1 box of your favorite 100% whole wheat or gluten free penne pasta, cooked
- ¾ cup good vodka
- 1 – 28 oz can diced tomatoes
- ¾ cup tomato paste
- ¾ cup water
- 3 cloves of roasted or minced garlic
- ½ cup red bell peppers, diced
- ¾ cup yellow onion, finely chopped
- 1 tbsp grapeseed oil (or water)
- 1 tsp balsamic vinegar
- ¼ tsp Kosher salt
- ½ tsp white or black pepper
- 1 tbsp nutritional yeast
- ¾ cup raw cashews (place in bowl with about ½ inch of water covering them and microwave 60 seconds)
- ½ cup fresh basil, torn
- 2 tbsp flat leaf parsley, chopped

Equipment: **serving bowl, dutch oven or large pot, wooden spoon/spatula, knife, measuring cup, measuring spoon, blender and whisk (optional)**

1. Add oil (or 3 tbsp of water if substituting) onions, salt and pepper to your pot, stir and cook over medium heat about 5 minutes or until translucent.
2. Add red peppers and garlic and cook, stirring frequently (to avoid garlic burning) for another 3 minutes.
3. Add tomato paste and cook, stirring frequently, for 3 minutes then add water, diced tomatoes, balsamic vinegar and vodka. Stir, reduce to low and cook 20 minutes uncovered, stirring frequently.
4. While the sauce is cooking, add the undrained cashews and the nutritional yeast to your high powered blender and blend on puree or high until it is completely smooth and creamy (no lumps) then set aside.
5. Scrape all your cashew sauce into your sauce pot, stir and cook another 5 minutes then taste, add any additional seasoning, toss into your large serving bowl with your pasta, top with basil and parsley and enjoy!

PROTEIN STUFFED PEPPERS

45 MINS

If you're looking for an easy make ahead that's great for lunch, dinner or leftovers, look no further than our Protein Stuffed Peppers! With beans, quinoa and a slew of other nutrient-rich ingredients, this protein-packed dish is easy to make and is brimming with flava!

SERVES 8

3 cups cooked quinoa
1 cup meatless crumbles (optional)
2 ½ cups black beans, rinsed and drained
1 cup baby bella or white mushrooms, chopped (optional)
6 large bell peppers (I prefer yellow or red)
1 cup yellow onions, diced
1 cup frozen yellow or white corn, thawed and rinsed
3 cloves of garlic, finely diced
3 tbsp tomato paste
¼ cup fresh cilantro roughly chopped
½ tsp garlic powder
½ tsp chili powder
½ tsp smoked paprika
½ tsp coriander
½ tsp cumin
½ tsp kosher salt (optional)
½ tsp pepper
⅛ tsp of aleppo or cayenne pepper
¼ tsp red pepper flakes (optional)
1 tbsp grapeseed oil

Equipment: Large mixing bowl, baking pan, parchment paper, measuring cups, measuring spoons, knife, spatula or wooden spoon, medium sized pot, large nonstick pan

1. Preheat oven to 400°F and line baking sheet with parchment paper and set aside.
2. After cleaning and drying your peppers, place them on their base/bottom and cut them in half horizontally, leaving the base of the outer stem intact then remove seeds and membrane in the two halves (leaving the stem base allows you to have to halves to fill – see corresponding picture).
3. Lightly rub oil inside and outside of peppers and place your peppers on the baking sheet and bake for 5-7 minutes then remove from oven and let them cool (goal is to soften a little, not cook).
4. Combine all dry spices (not cilantro) and set aside.
5. In a nonstick large pan over medium heat, add water (or 1 tbsp oil, if substituting), onions, and tomato paste and sauté 5 minutes, stirring frequently, then set aside in a bowl.
6. Add mushrooms to pan over medium heat with 1 tsp oil (or 1 tbsp of water, if substituting), 1 tsp blended seasonings and cook, stirring frequently, for about 5 minutes or until mushrooms have browned nicely, then set aside in the bowl with your onions and tomato paste.
7. Place pan over medium heat and add 1 tsp oil (or 1 tbsp water, if substituting) , crumbles and ¾ tsp of your dry spice, mix and cook 5 minutes (breaking up crumbles with wooden spoon and cooking to brown). Remove from heat, transfer to the bowl with the onions, mushrooms and tomato paste, and add the black beans and corn. Stir to combine and allow to cool 10 minutes in the fridge.
8. Remove bowl from fridge and add cilantro, another teaspoon of the dry spice blend, and cooked quinoa and gently fold to incorporate.
9. Divide stuffing mixture evenly among your peppers-packing it firmly to ensure each pepper is filled, then return filled peppers to baking pan and bake for 20–25 minutes oven uncovered or until quinoa is lightly browned on top then remove from oven, serve and enjoy!

LOADED VEGAN LOAF

75 MINS

Making the transition to a plant-based lifestyle was made easier once I learned that I could apply many of the same principles of animal-based cooking to my veggies. This vegan loaf is the perfect example of a familiar comfort dish that exceeds, not only because it's loaded with protein, fiber and nutrients, but because it's a familiar, satisfying dish that everyone will love!

SERVES 6

- 1 cup cooked brown lentils
- ½ cup cooked quinoa
- ¾ cup finely chopped yellow onion
- 3 cloves garlic, finely diced
- ½ cup celery finely chopped
- ½ cup grated carrots
- ¾ tsp garlic powder
- ½ tsp cayenne or aleppo pepper (optional)
- ¾ tsp oregano (dried)
- ½ tsp onion powder
- ¼ tsp kosher salt (optional)
- ½ tsp black pepper
- 3 tbsp nutritional yeast
- ¾ cup whole wheat or panko breadcrumbs
- 3 tbsp ground flaxseed
- 1 tbsp vegan Worcestershire sauce
- 1 tsp agave nectar
- 2 tbsp tomato paste mixed with 1 tbsp of water
- 2 tbsp tamari or liquid aminos
- 2 tbsp tahini
- 1 tbsp olive or grapeseed oil
- Herban Eats BBQ Sweet Agave Nectar BBQ Sauce (as glaze)

Equipment: **nonstick loaf pan, parchment paper (optional), large nonstick pan, large mixing bowl, spatula/spoon, knife, potato masher, measuring cup, measuring spoons, parchment paper (optional)**

1. Preheat oven to 375°F and prepare your loaf pan by lining with parchment paper and set aside..
2. Place a large pan over medium heat and add 1 tsp oil (or 1 tbsp water, if substituting), then add your onions, garlic, cayenne pepper and cook stirring frequently for 5 minutes or until translucent (if using water and it gets dry before it becomes translucent and add another teaspoon or two of water) and set aside in a large mixing bowl.
3. Place nonstick pan over medium heat and add oil (or 1 tbsp of water if substituting), celery, carrots, salt, dried oregano and black pepper. Stir frequently for about 7 minutes or until veggies become slightly tender, then remove from heat, transfer to a large bowl and allow to cool in fridge for 20 minutes.
4. Remove celery and carrot mixture from fridge and add nutritional yeast, flaxseed, lentils, ½ quinoa then give it a little mash (leaving it a little rustic) with gloved hands or potato masher. Then add all your wet ingredients (except the BBQ sauce), remaining quinoa and mix or fold to combine.
5. Add breadcrumbs to the mixing bowl, mix to combine then press the mixture firmly into loaf the pan, making certain that it's well-packed in all areas of the pan. Brush on a layer of your favorite Herban Eats BBQ sauce then bake covered with aluminum foil for 30 minutes. Remove from oven, add another layer of bbq sauce, then bake uncovered for 25 minutes; allowing at least 25 minutes to cool before cutting and enjoying!

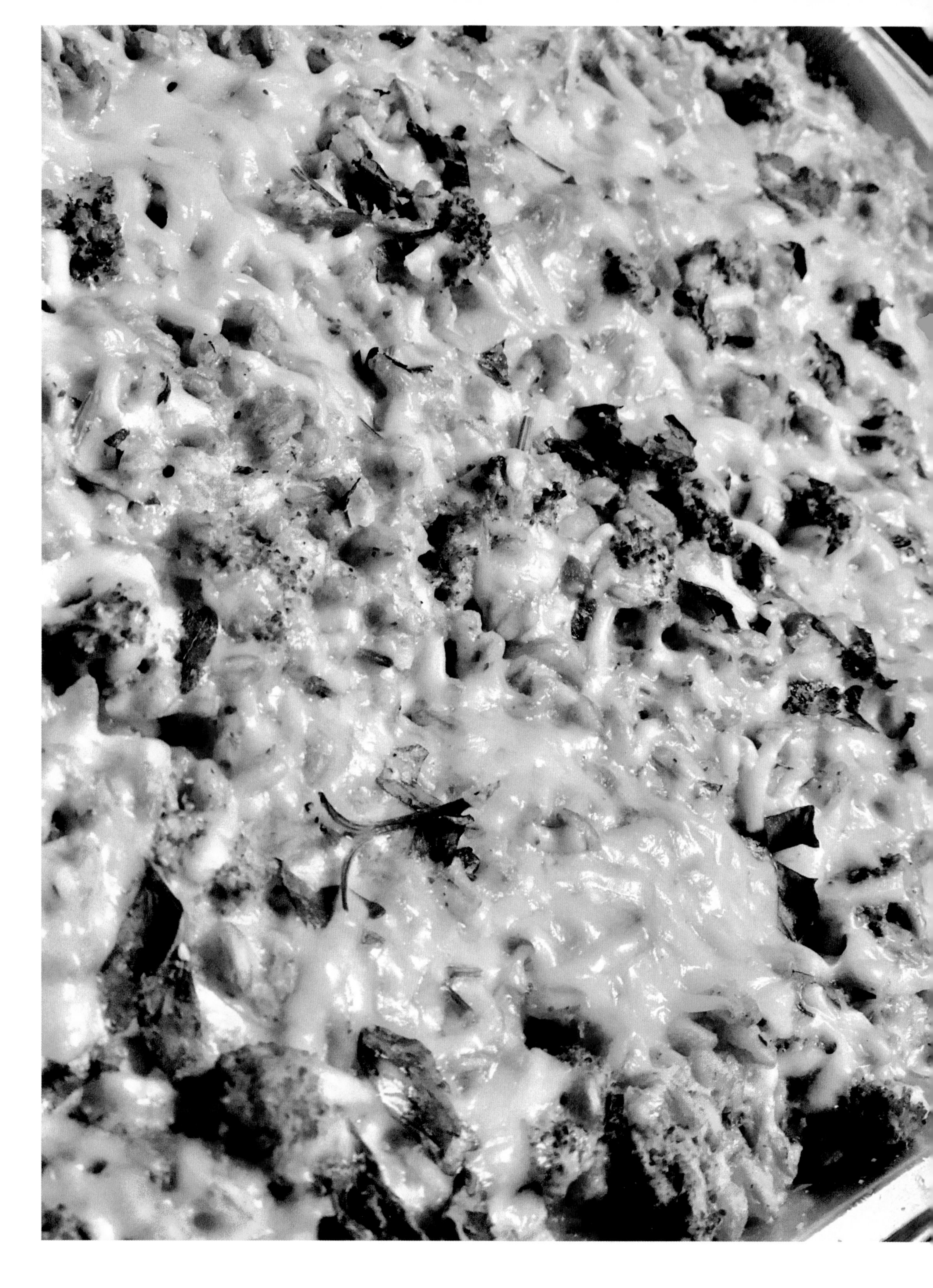

LOADED BROCCOLI & BROWN RICE CASSEROLE

60 MINS

Although she never knew it, my Great Aunt Willie Mae Boyd was my comfort food mentor and while we weren't kin by DNA, her kindness and our shared love for the kitchen made us more than in-laws. On weekend visits, I was lucky enough to have the opportunity to watch and sometimes assist with the Sunday breakfast and dinner, both of which she started at 4:30am and finished before heading off to Sunday school for the 5 adults and teens that resided under her roof. From the fresh greens sourced from her backyard, to her drop biscuits, Aunt Willie Mae put love on the plate and because of her I learned how to do the same. This recipe is my homage to my Aunt Willie Mae.

SERVES 8

- 2 cups broccoli florets, stemmed and cut in bite sized pieces
- 5 cups brown rice, cooked
- 1 ½ cups meatless crumbles
- 1 cup yellow onions, diced
- 2 cloves of garlic, minced
- ½ tsp black pepper
- 1 tsp salt (added to water to boil broccoli)
- ¾ tsp paprika
- 1 tbsp grapeseed oil (or water)
- 1 ½ cups whole wheat or panko bread crumbs
- ¼ cup flat leaf parsley, chopped
- 1 tbsp vegan butter or grapeseed oil (or water)
- ¾ cup shredded vegan mozzarella

FOR THE CHEESE SAUCE

- ⅓ cup nutritional yeast
- ½ cup raw cashews, soaked 2 hours, drained
- 2 ¼ cups unsweetened, unflavored soymilk or favorite plant milk
- ¾ tsp onion powder
- 1 tsp garlic powder
- ½ tsp black pepper
- ½ cup carrots, diced
- ½ cup red potatoes, peeled and diced
- 1 tbsp ground flaxseed
- 1 tbsp lemon juice
- ½ tsp agave (optional)
- ½ tsp siracha (optional)

Equipment: **large pot (or a pot and a double boiler) sauté pan, rectangular casserole pan (or two 9 inch square pans), parchment paper, knife, baking sheet, spatula, measuring spoons and cups, mixing spoons, 2 bowls, large bowl, high powered blender, strainer/colander**

1. Preheat oven to 400°F and prepare your casserole with light oil or parchment to avoid sticking.
2. Place broccoli in pot of boiling salted water for 5 minutes then drain and set aside.
3. Heat oil in a pan over medium heat (or 3 tablespoons of water if substituting) and cook the onions for 5 minutes or until translucent,. Add garlic and cook for another 3 minutes. Set aside in a bowl.
4. Add more oil to the pan (or 3 tablespoons of water if substituting) and brown the meatless crumbles (about 7 minutes), breaking them up with a wooden spoon and adding paprika and pepper. Add to the onions and garlic, combine and set aside.
5. Place carrots and potatoes in a pot, cover with water (about 2 cups water). Bring to a boil and cook until veggies are tender (about 10 minutes) then drain and add to the blender with all remaining cheese sauce ingredients then puree until smooth and set aside.
6. In a large bowl, add the cooked rice, broccoli, meatless crumbles and cheese sauce (reserving ½ cup for later use) and gently mix to combine (the consistency of the casserole should be more saucy than firm and should shake/jiggle easily), then pour into a casserole pan.
7. Pour the remaining cheese sauce over the top and smooth it evenly over your casserole with a spatula or spoon. Place aluminum foil over casserole, place on baking sheet and bake for 30 minutes.
8. For the casserole topping, mix together bread crumbs, vegan shredded cheese, parsley, oil (or 3 tablespoons of water if substituting) combine then sprinkle over the top of the casserole and return to the oven uncovered for 10 more minutes. Remove and allow to cool for 15 minutes before serving!

CURRY ROASTED CAULIFLOWER, KALE & POTATOES

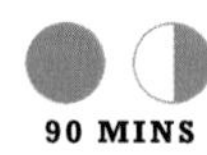

I was introduced to Indian food at an authentic, cozy restaurant in Charlotte NC called the Raga when I was 10 years old. One of my mom's favorite places, not only became one of mine but it also became one of my favorite cuisines. This recipe is my spin on memories of the Raga and everything I love about the simple beauty of Indian cuisine!

SERVES 8

- 4 cups cauliflower florets, no stems, chunky rough chopped
- 3 cups red potatoes, cubed ¼ to ½ inch
- 3 – 15 oz cans of unsweetened coconut milk
- 2 cups water
- 4 cups, baby spinach or baby kale, rough chopped
- 1 ½ cups yellow onions, diced
- ¾ cup fresh tomatoes, diced
- 3 cloves of garlic, roasted and minced
- 1 tsp fresh grated ginger or ½ tsp ground ginger
- ½ cup vegan sour cream, drained
- 1 tbsp grapeseed oil (or water)
- ¼ tsp garam masala
- ½ tsp cumin
- ½ tsp turmeric
- ¼ tsp coriander
- ½ tsp paprika
- 1 cinnamon stick
- ¾ tsp salt
- ½ tsp black or white pepper
- 1 ½ tsp Madras curry powder

Equipment: **dutch oven or large, deep pot, serving bowl, knife, measuring spoon and cups, can opener, wooden spoon, high powered blender or food processor, strainer/colander, large rimmed baking sheet, silpat or parchment paper**

1. Preheat oven to 400°F and prepare baking sheet with parchment or silpat.
2. Place cauliflower in large bowl, toss with oil (or ¼ cup water, if substituting), then spread evenly over baking sheet and place in oven for 25 minutes, turning halfway through the cooking process to ensure even cooking, then remove and set aside.
3. Put all the dried spices, onions, garlic and ginger into food processor and blend into a paste.
4. Place pot over medium heat, add paste and cook for 3 minutes until fragrant, adding a few tablespoons of water if needed.
5. Add fresh tomatoes, cinnamon stick, coconut milk, water and potatoes and stir. Once it comes to a rolling boil, drop heat to simmer, cover with fitted lid and cook for 20 minutes, making sure the potatoes are completely immersed.
6. Remove lid and add roasted cauliflower, stir and cook for another 15 minutes (lid on) so the cauliflower absorbs all the flavors.
7. Turn off heat and stir in the vegan sour cream and the chopped spinach.
8. Check for flavor and consistency, adjust accordingly, and serve over brown basmati rice.

ISLAND JACKFRUIT WRAP

30 MINS

When talking about flava there's just no getting around curry and curried dishes so we thought we'd give a nod to a non-traditional slider. With or without the wrap, this healthy this curry and coconut take on jackfruit eats like a meal while keeping the lunch boxes full and the dinner plates ready to roll after a long day's work!

SERVES 8

- 8–10 large wraps of your choice
- 4 cups jackfruit, shredded (if canned, rinsed, drained and shredded with food processer or fork)
- ¾ cups of leeks, cleaned, finely diced
- 3 cloves garlic, finely diced (optional)
- 2 cups coconut milk
- ½ cup cilantro, chopped
- 1 ½ tsp agave nectar (optional)
- ¼ tsp red pepper flakes (optional)
- ¾ tsp kosher or preferred salt
- 2 tbsp plus 1 tsp olive oil (or water substitution)

FOR THE CURRY SPICE MIX

- 2 tbsp ground cumin
- 2 tbsp ground mustard
- 1 tbsp ground thyme
- ¾ tsp cinnamon
- ¾ tsp ground ginger
- ½ tsp ground fenugreek
- 1 tsp ground cloves
- 1 tbsp ground allspice
- ¼ cup ground turmeric
- ¼ cup ground coriander

(Store extra curry spice mix in dry cool place for later use, this is more than you'll need for this recipe)

Equipment: dutch oven or large pan with lid, spatula/wooden spoon, knife, measuring cup, mixing bowl, measuring spoons, strainer/colander, food processer, parchment lined baking sheets, whisk

1. Preheat oven to 400°F and prepare your baking pans and set aside
2. Add all your mixed spices to a dry pan and toast them over a medium heat for one minute, whisking continuously until they release their fragrance. Remove from pan and set aside.
3. In a mixing bowl add the shredded jackfruit, 3 tbsp of toasted curry spice mix, toss with 1 tbsp olive oil (or 3 tbsp water if substituting), then distribute evenly across a baking sheet. Place in the center of the oven for 25 minutes then set aside.
4. In a mixing bowl add the leeks, garlic and 1 tbsp of the toasted curry spice mix, then combine with 1 tsp olive oil (or 3 tbsp water if substituting) and agave nectar, then distribute evenly across a baking sheet in the center of the oven for 15 minutes and set aside.
5. Place dutch oven or pot over medium heat and add coconut milk, jackfruit, leek and garlic mixture and stir to combine. Once combined, drop temperature to low, cover with fitted lid and let simmer for 20 minutes, stirring occasionally (should have consistency of pulled BBQ by end of cooking time).
6. Remove from heat and prepare to serve with a generous heap of our Purple Cabbage Slaw. (see page 75)

Wrap Directions

1. Place your wrap on a cutting board and evenly distribute on half of the wrap: a tablespoon of Purple Cabbage Slaw, ½ tsp of fresh cilantro and a heaped tbsp of jackfruit mix.
2. Roll the filled half of the wrap over to cover the filling, tuck the ends in tightly, and repeat until finished and enjoy!

TIP: For more flava, add ½ the toasted spice mix and ½ the coconut milk to a large ziplock bag with the uncooked jackfruit and let it marinate at least two hours in the fridge) then bring to room temp and follow step 3 in oven with jackfruit.

SMOKIN' SOUL BBQ JACKFRUIT SLIDERS

35 MINS

If you were ever a meat-eater, you likely ate or know many who ate BBQ, which is simply a common name for a smoked meat served in a variety of ways. When I ate BBQ, chopped BBQ was at the top of my list. Savory and delectable, this recipe introduces the same flavor profiles, without the guilt or risk factors for promotion of chronic disease!

SERVES 6

- 5 cups jackfruit, shredded (if canned, rinsed, drained and shredded with food processer or fork)
- 1 cup yellow onions, finely diced
- 3 cloves garlic, finely diced (optional)
- 1 ½ cups Herban Eats Smokin' Soul BBQ Sauce
- 1 tsp olive oil (optional)
- ¼ cup flat leaf parsley
- 1 ½ tsp olive oil (optional)
- ¾ tsp ground cumin
- ¾ tsp smoked paprika
- ½ tsp onion powder
- ¼ tsp ground coriander
- ¼ tsp black or white pepper

Equipment: **large pan with lid, spatula/wooden spoon, knife, measuring cup, mixing bowl, measuring spoons, strainer/colander, food processer, parchment lined baking sheets, whisk**

1. Preheat oven to 425°F and prepare your baking pan with parchment and set aside.
2. In a bowl, combine the cumin, paprika, onion powder, coriander and black or white pepper. Place a pan over medium-low heat, add mixed spices to the dry pan and whisk continuously to toast them for a minute or until they release their fragrance, then return to bowl and set aside.
3. In a large mixing bowl, add the shredded jackfruit, onions, toasted spices and olive oil (or 3 tbsp water if substituting), to combine, then place evenly on the baking sheet, bake for 25 minutes and set aside.
4. Place a large pan over medium heat and add the jackfruit with the Herban Eats BBQ Sauce and combine thoroughly.
5. Drop the temperature to low, place a tight fitting lid on the pan and allow to simmer for 15 minutes (stirring halfway through and checking for consistency).
6. Remove from heat, add parsley and serve with a generous heap of our Purple Cabbage Slaw (see page 75) atop your bun. Enjoy!

KRABBY CAKE SLIDERS

30 MINS

Among other things, I thoroughly enjoyed crab cakes with a simple remoulade. I once thought it had something to do with the crab, but it was really about the texture, flavor and how it was prepared since crab doesn't have a pronounced flavor. With hearts of palm as the base ingredient, this recipe gives me everything I like about crab cakes minus the crab!

SERVES 6

- 6 – vegan pretzel slider buns of your choice
- 2 cups hearts of palm, rinsed, drained and coarsely chopped with food processer
- ¼ cup chickpeas, rinsed, drained, and coarsely chopped in food processor
- 2 cloves garlic, minced
- ¼ cup yellow onion, finely diced
- ¼ cup red bell pepper, finely diced
- ½ cup vegan mayo
- 2 tsp stone ground mustard
- 1 tbsp fresh dill, finely chopped
- 1 tbsp flat leaf parsley
- 1 ½ tsp ground flaxseed
- 1 cup whole wheat bread crumbs or panko
- ½ tsp white pepper
- 1 ½ tsp old bay seasoning
- ¼ tbsp salt (optional)
- ¾ tsp dulse granules or nori flakes

Equipment: **large nonstick pan with a lid, spatula/wooden spoon, knife, measuring cup, mixing bowls, measuring spoons, strainer/colander, food processer, parchment lined baking sheets**

1. Preheat oven to 400°F and prepare your baking pan with parchment and set aside.
2. In a large mixing bowl, combine the hearts of palm, chickpeas, old bay seasoning flaxseed, dulse granules, white pepper and salt. Add vegan mayo, stone ground mustard, mix thoroughly then set aside in fridge.
3. In another mixing bowl, combine garlic, onions and peppers. Place a saute pan over medium-low heat then add the onion mixture and cook with a tight fitting lid for first minute (this will help render down and steam the onions, garlic and peppers more quickly). Remove lid and cook another 3 minutes. Remove from heat, and place your cooked veggies on a plate or bowl and set aside in fridge for 15 minutes to cool.
4. Remove both the hearts of palm mixture and the onion mixture from fridge and add the onion mixture, dill, parsley and bread crumbs to the bowl with your hearts of palm and combine.
5. Once combined, make golf ball sized rounds (remember these are for slider buns), then form into patties, place on your prepared baking pan for oven or a plate for pan cooking and repeat until finished.
6. **If baking:** place patties on lined baking sheet in 400°F oven for 25 minutes (turning halfway through).

   If pan cooking: place in small batches of 3 in small pan over medium high heat and with a tbsp of oil, then cook patties 4 minutes a side. Place on a kitchen or paper towel to remove any excess oil or put on baking sheet in the center rack of a 450°F oven for 4 minutes a side to get them good and crispy, then enjoy!

BBQ BLACK BEAN SLIDERS

25 MINS

$

Once you've ditched the animal products, there's nothing better than the satisfaction of building a great burger! Loaded with protein and fiber, this black bean slider is a guaranteed flava winner that can be made-ahead, frozen or served right away!

SERVES 6

- 6 – vegan pretzel slider buns of your choice
- 3 – 15 oz cans of black beans, rinsed and drained
- ¼ cup zucchini, diced
- ¼ cup yellow onion
- ¾ cup cooked brown rice
- ¼ cup raw walnuts
- ¼ cup raw pumpkin seeds
- ¼ cup almonds
- ¾ cup whole wheat bread crumbs or panko
- 1 flax egg (1 tbsp flax meal and 3 tbsp water, mixed and rested for 5 mins)
- ½ tsp ground cumin
- ¾ tsp garlic powder
- ½ tsp ground coriander
- ¾ tsp smoked paprika
- ½ tsp ground black pepper
- ½ tsp kosher or preferred salt (optional)
- 2 tbsp flat leaf parsley, finely chopped
- 3 ½ tbsp Herban-Eats Smokin' Soul Vegan BBQ Sauce

AVOCADO SPREAD

- ⅛ cup fresh cilantro, chopped
- 2 avocados, mashed
- ¾ tsp lime juice
- ½ tsp lime zest
- ¼ tsp black pepper
- a pinch of kosher or preferred salt
- 1 tbsp grapeseed oil (optional, water can be substituted)

Equipment: **large pan, mixing bowls (1 large, 1 small), spatula/spoon, knife, measuring cup, measuring spoons, potato masher, strainer/colander, food processer, parchment lined baking sheet (if not cooking on grill or stovetop)**

1. Preheat oven to 400°F and prepare your baking pan and set aside.
2. Mix dried spices together and set aside.
3. Spread your black beans evenly along your baking sheet, drizzle with a little olive oil, salt and pepper, place on center oven rack for 10 minutes then set aside in large mixing bowl.
4. Place a pan on medium with ½ tsp of oil (or 2 tbsp of water if substituting) and add onions and zucchini to the pan and cook for about 5 minutes or until veggies have gotten tender, then place in strainer and set aside.
5. Place all the nuts and seeds in the food processor, season with ¼ tsp of your spice blend and pulse a few times then add the nut mixture to the large mixing bowl.
6. Add half of the beans and all of the cooked zucchini and onion mix to food processer and pulse until its roughly combined and a little mushy then add it to the large mixing bowl with your nuts. Add remaining fresh herbs, spices, bbq sauce, flax egg, bread crumbs, cooked brown rice or quinoa and mix to incorporate all ingredients (If mixture is too wet to form a good ball, add a little more bread crumb).
7. Make a tight ball a bit larger than a golf ball, then form your patties on a plate or tray. Once you've made your sliders, place them in the fridge for at least 20 minutes.
8. Remove the sliders from fridge and allow them to sit for 5 minutes until they have returned to room temperature. Place large nonstick pan over medium heat and add a teaspoon of oil (optional). Cook sliders for 3–4 minutes a side (add a teaspoon of oil to each new batch. and repeat for subsequent batches. You could also place sliders on a prepared baking sheet and place in 400°F oven for 7 minutes a side then enjoy!

Avocado Spread Recipe

In a mixing bowl, combine all of the ingredients for the avocado spread, mix with a fork or quick pulses in the food processer and enjoy!

RECIPES

$ $25 OR LESS $$ $26 OR MORE

"OUR GREATEST WHY" HE

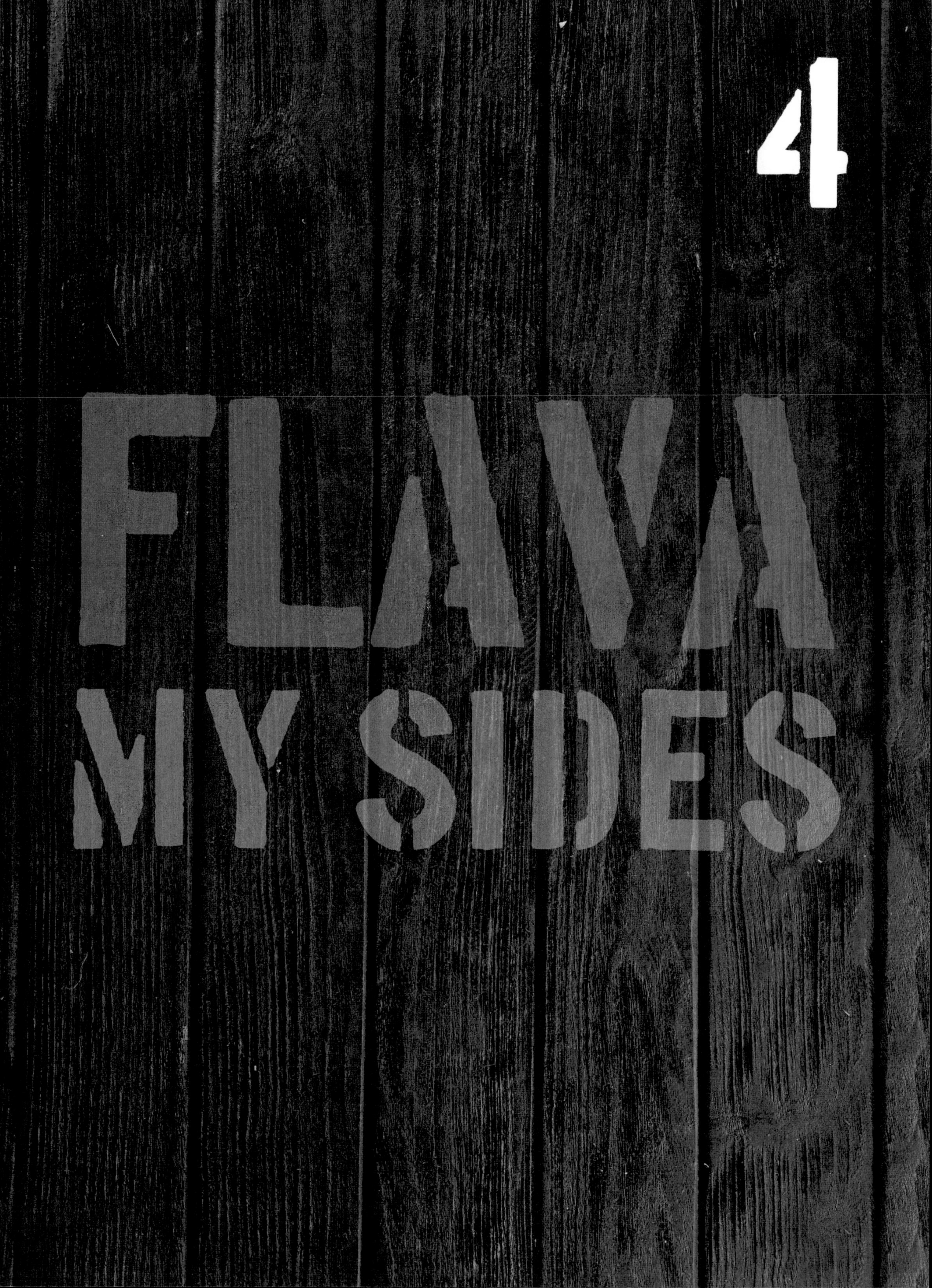
4
FLAVA
MY SIDES

ROASTED BALSAMIC BRUSSELS SPROUTS

30 MINS

I grew up hating brussels sprouts! As adorable as they looked, most people I knew prepared them boiled and whole, leaving them bitter and flavorless. As an adult who loved cooking, I learned to make these cute little cruciferous treats in a variety of ways and everyone who eats them this way falls in love with them!

SERVES 6

- 3 cups of brussels, cut in half lengthwise
- 2 leeks rinsed and chopped
- 1 tbsp grapeseed oil (or water)
- 3 tbsp balsamic vinegar
- 2 tbsp balsamic glaze
- ½ tsp Kosher salt
- ½ tsp ground black pepper
- ¾ tsp garlic powder

Equipment: **mixing bowl, sheet pan with silpat or parchment paper (optional), mixing spoon, knife, measuring cup, measuring spoon**

1. Preheat the oven to 425°F, and prepare your baking pan with silpat or parchment.
2. In a mixing bowl, place your chopped Brussels (including the loose leaves; they get crispy with roasted) and add salt, pepper, garlic powder, chopped leeks, and oil (or 3 tbsp water if substituting) then toss to combine to evenly distribute the spices.
3. Evenly spread a single layer of your Brussels (facing down on the pan).
4. Place pan on middle rack of oven and bake for 25 minutes, adding the balsamic vinegar when you are turning halfway through the cook time.
5. Remove from oven, and evenly distribute the balsamic glaze while still on baking pan, place back in oven 5 more minutes, remove, place in serving dish, and enjoy!

CURRY ROASTED CABBAGE

45 MINS

$

From southern soul to Indian iterations, cabbage is a versatile, vitamin-filled chameleon that loves soaking in flavor! So, we thought we'd add a little island flair with this quick and easy Caribbean curry dish that the whole family will enjoy!

SERVES 6

2 heads of cabbage, shredded or chopped (about 5 cups)
2 cups of leeks, cleaned and chopped
3 – 15 oz cans of unsweetened coconut milk
½ cup water
1 tbsp olive or grapeseed oil
¼ cup flat leaf parsley, chopped
3 tbsp curry powder
2 tsp turmeric
¾ tsp allspice
¾ tsp coriander
1 tsp garlic powder
½ tsp black pepper
a pinch of cayenne pepper
¾ tsp kosher salt

Equipment: **mixing bowl, large baking sheet with parchment paper, spatula/spoon, knife, measuring cup, measuring spoons, whisk, large ziploc bags, lidded bowl**

1. With the exception of the parsley, whisk all your spices, coconut milk, water and divide evenly into two ziploc bags.
2. Add shredded cabbage and leeks evenly to both ziploc bags, filling no more than ¾ full. Seal bags, then move coconut mixture throughout bag and set aside in fridge for at least 60 minutes (the longer it marinates, the more flavorful it becomes).
3. Preheat oven to 425°F, remove cabbage bags from fridge and bring to room temperature.
4. Strain your cabbage in a colander, placing a bowl beneath it to reserve the leftover marinade and set coconut marinade aside.
5. Evenly distribute cabbage to lined baking sheets, place in oven for 30 minutes (making sure to check and turn it on the baking sheet halfway through the cooking time).
6. In a large lidded container or bowl, add the curried cabbage and the leftover marinade, put on the lid and shake or combine until it's evenly distributed.
7. Change parchment paper, redistribute cabbage onto lined baking sheets and place in the oven for another 20 minutes. Remove from oven, add parsley, toss, serve and enjoy!

SMASHED CAULIFLOWER

30 MINS

Counting carbs or calories has never been my thing but for those who either enjoy or have a habit of counting, this smashed cauliflower side dish is a delectable easy and nutrient-dense way to enjoy the potato-feel, without having to concern yourself with counting!

SERVES 4

- 1 large head of cauliflower chopped into florets (yield 2 ½ cups)
- 2 roasted garlic cloves finely chopped (or ½ tsp garlic powder to substitute)
- 1 ½ tsp grapeseed oil (optional)
- 1 tbsp fresh chives, chopped
- 1 tbsp fresh dill, chopped
- zest of ½ a lemon
- ¼ tsp pepper
- ½ tsp salt (for the cooking water)
- ¼ cup low sodium vegetable stock
- 2 tbsp vegan cream cheese

Equipment: large pot, zester, large pan, bowls (1 large, 1 small), spatula/spoon, knife, measuring cup, measuring spoons, potato masher, strainer/colander

1. Fill a pot with water, salt the water (like the ocean-optional) and once water comes to a light rolling boil, add the cauliflower for 10 minutes or until it's just slightly fork tender (not soft or mushy).
2. Drain the cauliflower in a strainer and place back in the pot.
3. Add the roasted garlic cloves (or ½ tsp garlic powder), vegan cream cheese, stock, and pepper then smash roughly with a potato masher until your desired texture is reached (I like it a little chunky).
4. Add fresh herbs, lemon zest , gently combine, taste for flavor and consistency and enjoy!

CREAMY CORN

30 MINS

While derivatives of corn such as: corn syrup and corn oil are wildly unhealthy, corn in its' whole form is high in fiber, vitamins, minerals and nutrients. This quick and comforting corn dish is a side that helps make the transition to a plant-based vegan lifestyle easy, affordable and amazingly good.

SERVES 6

6 ears of corn, husked and silked
1 small onion, finely diced
3 tbsp fresh dill, chopped
1 tsp agave nectar
2 tbsp vegan cream cheese (optional)
1 tsp vegan butter (optional)
¼ cup low sodium veg stock or water
¾ cup unsweetened, unflavored soy milk (or almond milk)
½ tsp salt (optional)
¾ tsp garlic powder
½ tsp black pepper
½ tsp smoked paprika

Equipment: large pot or dutch oven, spatula/spoon, knife, measuring cup, measuring spoons, bowl

1. Cut tips off one side of your corn so it will remain flat and stable on your cutting board or nestled in your bowl then remove corn from cob with your knife, place in a bowl and set aside.
2. Take the corn cobs and with the back of your knife or a spoon, scrape up and down the cob and collect the milk (the white substance that comes off of the cob when scraped) from each ear and add the collected milk to your bowl of corn.
3. Warm pot over medium heat and add oil (or water).
4. Add onions, all your spices and cook, stirring every minute for about 5 minutes or until onions are translucent.
5. With the exception of the dill and the vegan cream cheese, add all the remaining ingredients, stir to combine, cover with lid and drop temperature to a low simmer for 20 minutes (checking halfway through to ensure there's enough liquid and to check for doneness).
6. Remove from heat, check for flavor and consistency, add vegan cream cheese, dill, stir to combine, serve and enjoy!

SMOKIN COLLARDS

45 MINS

As a soulful girl, it should go without saying that I also enjoy that same thing on my plate every now and then. In my community, other than mac & cheese, nothing says soul more than a good plate of collards. So, it was important for me to get the smoky in my greens minus the use of animal necks and wings. I also never like stalky stems anywhere close to my greens because they make for uneven cooking, slow cooking time and don't absorb flavor as easily as the leaves themselves do. Enjoy our nod to a comforting, nutrient dense, yummy, flava-filled winner!

SERVES 6

- 4 large bunches of collard greens, cleaned, no large or medium stems, chopped evenly
- 1 cup yellow onion, finely chopped
- 3 garlic cloves, minced (or 1 tbsp garlic powder)
- 1 ½ tbsp liquid smoke
- 1 tbsp tamari or liquid aminos
- 1 ½ tsp grapeseed oil (or water)
- 1 ½ tbsp smoked paprika
- 3 tbsp apple cider vinegar
- 2 ½ cups water
- 2 tsp pepper
- ½ tsp salt (optional)
- ¾ tsp agave nectar (optional)
- 1 tbsp vegan butter (optional)

Equipment: large pot or dutch oven and lid, spatula/spoon, knife, measuring cup, measuring spoons

1. Warm pot over medium heat and add oil (3 tbsp of water if substituting).
2. Add onions, ¾ tsp smoked paprika, 1 tsp pepper and salt (optional). Combine and cook about 5 minutes or until onions are translucent.
3. Add garlic, and cook for 3 minutes then add all your liquids and bring to a boil.
4. Add greens, vegan butter and remaining dry seasonings, reduce heat to simmer, place your lid on and cook for 30 minutes (stirring every 10 minutes and checking for pot gravy – may have to add more water by the ¼ cup).
5. Greens will be tender and ready about 30–40 minutes without the large stems. Remove from heat, check for seasoning, adjust accordingly and enjoy!

EASY PURPLE CABBAGE SLAW

25 MINS

When settling in for a good meal, the two things that I'm expecting, beyond flava, are lots of vibrant colors and tons of texture. With a plant-based vegan lifestyle, those options are endless. While crunchy cabbage fits the bill, bringing in the deep purple cabbage, not only gives me the texture and nutrients that I want but it also brings even more vital antioxidants and anti-inflammatory properties to the plate.

SERVES 4

FOR THE SLAW

3 cups purple cabbage, cored and shredded (one large head of cabbage)
1 ½ cup carrots, shredded
¾ cup green onions, chopped
¼ cup flat leaf parsley
1 cup cranberries, chopped and reconstituted

FOR THE DRESSING

1 tsp unfiltered apple cider vinegar
1 ½ tbsp of Dijon mustard
¾ tsp kosher or preferred salt
¾ tsp ground black pepper
⅓ cup vegan mayonnaise

Equipment: **knife, serving bowl measuring spoon, measuring cup, gloves**

1. Add the vinegar, vegan mayo, mustard and agave nectar with the salt and pepper to the cabbage and shredded carrots, in a bowl.
2. Blend to combine with a spoon, then with a gloved hand, massage the ingredients into the cabbage until it begins to break down (like curly kale, cabbage is hard to break down without massaging it).
3. Add in the green onions, fresh herbs and cranberries, stir to combine then allow at least 30 minutes in the refrigerator until ready to use.

CHUNKY RED POTATO SMASH WITH SAWMILL GRAVY

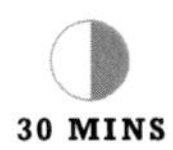

30 MINS

$

If you're looking for home, this comforting, feel-good bonanza of all things soulful and familiar is your ticket to ride. Seemingly simple, it's easy to overwork and under season a simple dish like the gravy. We have paired the potatoes with the gravy here but you can use this with any number of included recipes like our meatloaf or perfect breakfast hash. Try doubling the recipe here and be ready to have no leftovers, no matter how much you make; it's just that good.

SERVES 6

- 6–8 red potatoes (cleaned and cut into equal quarters or small cubes for faster cooking time)
- 3 garlic cloves, roasted or minced
- ⅓ cup plant milk
- 1 tbsp grapeseed oil or plant butter (optional)
- 2 tsp kosher salt (for water boiling-optional)
- 1 sprig of fresh rosemary

FOR THE SAWMILL GRAVY

- ¾ cup all purpose or whole wheat flour
- ¼ cup yellow onion, finely chopped
- 4 cups unflavored, unsweetened soy or almond milk
- 2 tsp plant butter or grapeseed oil (optional or 3 tsp water)
- 1 package meatless crumbles
- ¼ tsp Kosher salt
- ¾ tsp ground sage
- ½ tsp ground black pepper
- ½ tsp garlic powder
- ¼ tsp smoked paprika

Equipment: large mixing or serving bowl, large pot, large pan or strainer/colander, small pot, potato masher, mixing spoons, knife, measuring cups, wooden and measuring spoons

1. Add your evenly cut potatoes to a large pot, cover with about an inch of cold salted water, bring to a boil and cook for about 15 minutes (At the 10 minute mark, check the potatoes. If the knife easily pierces the potato, they are ready for removal).
2. While potatoes are boiling, add optional vegan butter/oil to another pot over medium heat with garlic and cook for about 3 minutes. Drop temperature to low add plant milk, rosemary sprig and let simmer, stirring intermittently with a wooden spoon for about 7 minutes. Remove rosemary sprig and set aside mixture to cool for about 10 minutes (or fridge for 5 minutes).
3. Drain the potatoes in a colander, set aside for a couple minutes, then return to the pot for a rough mash (do not over mash, leave some rustic chunky bits, which work well when adding in milk mixture). Place in a large mixing bowl.
4. Once the potatoes have cooled, pour the plant milk mixture over them (do not overmix, just combine), cover and set aside.
5. Add about a teaspoon of your chosen oil along with the onions to large pan and cook over medium heat for about 5 minutes or until translucent, then remove from pan and set aside in a bowl.
6. Add a teaspoon of oil to the pan and cook your crumbles and your dried seasonings over medium heat for 4–5 minutes, breaking up the crumbles with a wooden spoon, making sure to combine well, until starting to brown.
7. Add the onions back to pan and the flour. Combine well and cook for 4 minutes (it is important that floured crumbles and mixture receive direct heat from pan; not just covering top of mixture).
8. Reduce temperature to simmer/low, stir in plant milk ½ cup at a time, waiting for the mixture to thicken (if too thick add a little more plant milk, one tablespoon at a time or water if you prefer).
9. Remove from heat, check for flavor and consistency, pour over your potatoes and enjoy!

RECIPES

$ $25 OR LESS $$ $26 OR MORE

"OUR GREATEST WHY" HE Dawn Hilton-Williams

5

FLAVA

MY BREAKFAST

FLUFFY PANCAKES

After months of being the queen of all varieties of oats, cereals and seeds, I decided it was time to figure out how to make a great breakfast staple that was neither loaded with fats nor frozen (but are both freezable and microwaveable). This recipe is an easy nod to the familiar and feels like home in every way.

MAKES 6

- 2 cups unbleached all-purpose flour (or wheat flour)
- 4 tbsp organic cane sugar
- 2 tbsp baking powder
- ¼ tsp ground cinnamon
- ½ tsp kosher salt or other salt (not sea salt)
- 2 cups unsweetened, unflavored plant milk (soy, cashew or almond)
- 2 tbsp vanilla extract
- 2 tbsp apple cider vinegar

Equipment: large mixing bowl, small mixing bowl, spatula, large saute coated or griddle, whisk, spoon, measuring cups and measuring spoons

1. In a large mixing bowl, add the flour, sugar, baking powder, cinnamon and salt and whisk to combine.
2. In a separate bowl, combine the plant milk, vanilla extract, apple cider vinegar, stir to combine and set aside for about 5 minutes (this makes a vegan buttermilk).
3. Pour the vegan buttermilk into the bowl of dry ingredients and mix with a mixing spoon, then set aside.
4. Preheat the stovetop to a medium heat (or 275°F on a electric griddle), then pour in a scoop of about ¼ cup per pancake or whatever size you enjoy.
5. Once you see you bubbles dotting the pancake, you know its time to flip (about 2 minutes per side) then cook the other side. Serve with fresh berries or sliced bananas and Grade A maple syrup.

TIP: Double the recipe and freeze your pancakes for later! Good for up to 3 months in freezer and 1 week in fridge.

BANANA NUT BREAD

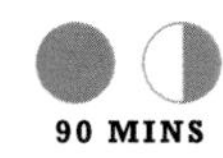

$

When you're in a hurry and and on the go, this is an easy recipe that really shows off the simple substitutions that make vegan cooking so easy, affordable and delicious!

SERVES 8

- 2 cups unbleached all-purpose flour
- ¾ cup of organic raw cane sugar
- 1 tsp baking soda
- a pinch of ground cinnamon
- ¼ tsp Kosher Salt or other salt
- 2 tbsp ground flaxseed (mixed into 5 ½ tbsp water)
- ⅓ cup organic soy or other plant milk
- 1 tsp vanilla extract
- ½ cup melted coconut oil or canola (I prefer coconut)
- 3 large bananas, mashed (just overripe is perfect-mash with potato masher, fork or by pulsing in your food processor)

Equipment: large mixing bowl, small mixing bowl, spatulas, favorite bread pan (9 x 5 is ideal) or loaf pan, colander, measuring cups & measuring spoons, parchment paper, whisk

1. Preheat oven to 350°F and line your loaf or casserole with parchment paper.
2. In a large bowl whisk together flour, baking soda, cinnamon, salt and sugar.
3. Add the flaxseed mixture, plant milk, vanilla extract, oil and mashed bananas to the large bowl and mix to incorporate.
4. Fold in your chopped walnuts (do not overmix just fold to combine).
5. Pour into parchment lined pan (parchment will move around a bit but can be adjusted once the mixture is poured in).
6. Place in the oven for about 60 minutes or until your toothpick is clean when tested in center of your loaf.
7. Remove and let cool in pan for 15 minutes before placing onto a cooling rack.

HEARTY BREAKFAST HASH

35 MINS

My Grandpa Caesar was a big fan of corned beef hash; always fixing it for me for breakfast. Naturally, I grew up enjoying it, in part, because of those memories. While not quite the same, this play on a vegan-meaty hash takes me back to my grandpa's table with lots of flava and warmth on the plate.

SERVES 4

- 6 red potatoes diced small (4 cups)
- 1 cup meatless crumbles
- 1 tbsp grapeseed oil (or water)
- 1 cup onions, diced
- ¼ cup yellow and ¼ cup red bell peppers, diced
- 2 garlic cloves, minced
- ¼ cup flat leaf parsley, chopped
- 2 ½ tsp smoked paprika
- ¼ tsp coriander
- ¾ tsp kosher salt (optional)
- ½ tsp black pepper
- ¾ tsp garlic powder
- 1 ½ tsp agave nectar

Equipment: **large nonstick pan, knife, measuring spoons, measuring cups, wooden spoon or spatula, large baking pan/sheet, parchment paper**

1. Preheat oven to 425°F and prepare baking sheet with parchment for potatoes.
2. In a large bowl, season potatoes with a tbsp of oil (or 3 tbsp water), ½ tsp salt, ¼ tsp garlic powder, ¼ tsp coriander and 1 ¼ tsp smoked paprika, then place on a baking sheet in the middle of the oven and bake for 30 minutes (turning halfway through cooking time to ensure even browning/cooking), then remove and set aside in a large bowl.
3. Place pan over medium to medium high heat and add a teaspoon of oil (or 1 tbsp water if substituting).
4. Once pan is warm, break up the meatless crumbles with your wooden or pan safe spoon, add the 1 ¼ tsp paprika, garlic powder, and ½ tsp black pepper and cook for about 5 minutes until brown, then set aside.
5. Heat a tsp of oil in a pan (or 3 tbsp water if substituting), and sauté the onions, peppers, fresh garlic, ¼ tsp salt (optional) for about 5 minutes or until the onions are translucent then add, along with the prepared meatless crumbles, to the bowl with potatoes, being careful not to mash up the potatoes.
6. Once combined, add to baking sheet, spreading out as evenly as possible and bake for another 10 minutes. Remove from oven, place in bowl, add your parsley, toss, then garnish top with smoked paprika and enjoy!

LOADED VEGAN OMELETTES

30 MINS

I have tried a few vegan omelette recipes but the base has to be perfect and because of Chef GW Chew (Veg Hub & Something Better Foods), I was able to put a little of my own spin on his great vegan omelette recipe. My family requests this delicious tofu & rolled oats winner every weekend!

SERVES 6

FOR THE BATTER

2 cups rolled oats
2 cups of drained and crumbled organic tofu (can be firm or extra firm)
2 cups water

FOR THE ESSENTIAL FLAVA MIX

This is used to season the tofu before it is blended and is used to enhance the batter
2 cups nutritional yeast
1 tsp salt
1 tsp white pepper
¾ tsp onion powder
1 tsp garlic powder
¾ tsp smoked paprika
1 tbsp turmeric
¼ tsp dulse granules (optional)

FOR THE FILLING

1 ½ cups meatless crumbles
2 – 9 oz bags of spinach, chopped
¾ cup yellow onion, finely diced
2 tbsp all-purpose flour
¼ cup water
½ tsp pepper
¼ tsp garlic powder
¼ tsp smoked paprika
½ tsp salt (optional)

1 cup of shredded vegan cheese (optional)

Equipment: large mixing bowl, small mixing bowl, spatula, saute pan, griddle, blender, measuring cups & measuring spoons

1. Add to your blender, tofu, rolled oats and ½ cup of essential flava mix then blend, adding ½ cup of water at a time until the mixture becomes a smooth batter.
2. Taste for flavor and adjust accordingly by adding, if necessary, more of the Essential Flava Mix, then set aside.
3. Place nonstick pan over medium heat, add oil (or 3 tbsp water if substituting), onion and cook about 5 minutes or until onion becomes translucent. Add flour, combine with onions and cook another two minutes, stirring constantly. Add meatless crumbles (breaking up and integrating with onion-flour mixture with wooden or pan-safe spoon), season with salt, garlic powder, pepper and paprika for 5 minutes. Remove from pan and set aside.
4. Place pan and ¼ cup water over medium heat. Add chopped spinach, stir, cover with tight fitting lid and allow it to cook down about 3 minutes. Add back your onion and crumbles mixture, and combine; this is your filling!
5. Set your griddle to 275°F and let it warm (if your griddle isn't non-stick, you will need to use a cooking spray to prevent the omelette from sticking). Pour your batter onto the griddle or pan and spread it outward a little bit (making sure the batter is evenly distributed in a circle. Like a pancake (but flatter and faster), you will see some change in color and perhaps a bubble or two. Once the batter color changes (about 45 seconds if your griddle is right temp and your batter isn't too thick) add a teaspoon of cheese and your crumbles and spinach mixture to one side of your omelette, allow to cook about 45 seconds, then fold the other half of your omelette over to cover the filling. Give it a good tap to smash it down a little, wait about 30 seconds, then gently turn omelette.
6. Once flipped, allow the other side and the center to cook. Repeat flipping every 30 seconds (giving it a gentle tap/smash after each flip) this will allow the time needed for center and sides to cook. Repeat the flipping until it is a bit crusty and cooked (about 3 flips per side should do it) then set aside and repeat the process for the next omelette then enjoy!

RECIPES

$ $25 OR LESS $ $ $26 OR MORE

"OUR GREATEST WHY" HE

6

FLAVA

MY DESSERTS

CARROT CAKE WITH VEGAN CREAM CHEESE FROSTING

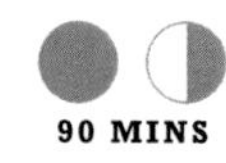

90 MINS

Never the biggest fan of carrot cake, I toyed with different recipes over the years. It wasn't until I became plant-based that I was able to create a carrot cake that I could really get behind and share with clients, family and friends!

SERVES 10

2 ½ cups unbleached all-purpose flour
1 cup packed light brown sugar
1 cup white granulated or organic cane sugar
2 tsp ground cinnamon ground
1 tsp baking soda
1 tsp Kosher or table salt (not sea salt)
¼ tsp ground nutmeg
1 cup raw walnuts either rough-chopped or well-pulsed in food processor
3 cups carrots, grated (or get the pre-packaged shredded ones and pulse in food processor or chop them)
½ cup canola oil
1 cup unsweetened, unflavored applesauce
¾ cup unsweetened, unflavored soy milk (you can also use, almond, hazelnut or cashew milk)
1 tbsp vanilla extract

VEGAN CREAM CHEESE FROSTING

½ cup room temperature softened vegan butter
8 oz vegan cream cheese
1 ¼ tsp vanilla extract
4 cups powdered or confectioners sugar

Equipment: large mixing bowl, smaller bowls, measuring cups, measuring spoons, two 9 inch square baking dishes or two round 8 inch pans, parchment paper, whisk, mixing spoon, grater, chef's knife, hand or standing mixer

1. Preheat the oven to 350°F and prepare your baking pans with parchment or light cooking spray.
2. Place the flour in a large bowl, then mix in the sugar (white and brown), cinnamon, baking soda, salt and nutmeg.
3. In a separate, smaller bowl, mix the oil, applesauce, soy milk and vanilla extract.
4. Pour the wet ingredients into the dry ingredients bowl and mix until combined, then add your walnuts and carrots and fold until well combined.
5. Pour the batter evenly into the two pans and bake on middle rack for 40 minutes (clean toothpick and set cake tops mean they are ready to come out of the oven).
6. Allow the cake to cool in baking pans at least 15 minutes then transfer to a cooling rack.

Vegan Cream Cheese Frosting Recipe

1. In large mixing bowl, add the softened vegan butter and beat with mixer until creamy.
2. Add your vegan cream cheese and beat for 1 minute to combine with the butter.
3. Add the vanilla then the sugar (a cup at a time), all the while continuing to beat on a low speed until smooth (it may not look thick at this point but it will thicken in the refrigerator so don't panic).
4. Spread over your cooled cake and allow frosting to set on cake in the fridge for 30 minutes, then serve and enjoy!

EASY BLUEBERRY NICE CREAM

15 MINS

As prep and ingredients go, it doesn't get easier, tastier or figure-friendly than this! All you need is a freezer, a good blender or food processer and a few minutes and you are on your way to impressing somebody with this yummy vegan treat!

SERVES 4

5 ripe or overripe bananas, cut into chunks, bagged and frozen
1 ¼ cups, blueberries, frozen

FOR THE TOPPINGS
fresh mint, chopped
chopped walnuts or almonds
fresh blueberries

Equipment: large lidded freezer friendly bowl, high powered blender (I prefer food processer), freezer, spoons and ice cream scooper

1. Add frozen bananas and blueberries to your blender or processer and puree, pulse or blend-stopping intermittently to scrape down the sides.
2. Once lump-free and creamy, put your nice cream in a freezer-safe, lidded container for at least 30 minutes then scoop, serve, top and enjoy!

MEYER LEMON COOKIES

25 MINS

Light, easy and fun, these lemony delights are the perfect finish for any spring or summer meal. It's also an excellent way to introduce a vegan treat to family and friends!

MAKES 25

¾ cup vegan butter, melted
½ cup meyer lemon juice
and the zest of ½ of the lemon
1 tsp vanilla extract
1 tsp lemon extract
1 ½ cups organic cane sugar
¼ tsp kosher salt
a pinch of ground cinnamon
2 ½ cups unbleached all-purpose
pre-sifted flour
1 tbsp baking powder

Equipment: **large mixing bowl, spoon, whisk, parchment paper, lemon zester, baking sheet, measuring cups & measuring spoons**

1. Preheat your oven to 350°F and line your baking sheet with parchment paper.
2. Mix dry stuff together and whisk until combined.
3. In a separate bowl, mix wet stuff to combine and then pour wet stuff into the dry and stir until evenly combined.
4. Spoon out tablespoon-sized portions of cookie dough on to prepared baking sheets, then place on center oven rack for 10 minutes.
5. Remove from oven, allow to rest on baking sheet for 5 to 10 minutes then serve and enjoy!

PURPLE SWEET POTATO PIE

75 MINS

My Grandpa Lester Hilton, much like my father, Larry, had his own recipes for his best dishes and at some point, his sweet potato pie recipe was passed down to me. As delicious as it was, I had to make some healthy but soulful changes. From changing the potato (yes, purple sweet potatoes are a real, non-gmo thing), to changing the sugars and dairy, this low Glycemic Index treat, is loaded with all the antioxidants, beta carotene, and vitamins you can handle! My father and Grandpa Lester may be gone, but a sweet piece of them lives on in this soulful recipe.

SERVES 8

- 1–2 packs of prepared deep dish (9 inch) vegan pie crust(s)
- 4 medium or 3 large purple sweet potatoes, washed and cleaned (to yield 2 ½ cups of cooked potatoes)
- 1 cup unsweetened, unflavored soymilk
- ½ cup agave nectar
- ¼ cup vegan butter, room temp
- ¾ tsp vanilla extract
- ½ tsp ground nutmeg
- ½ tsp ground cinnamon
- ¼ tsp ground ginger
- 2 ½ tbsp cornstarch
- ¼ tsp kosher salt

FOR THE TOPPING (OPTIONAL)

- ¼ cup chopped walnuts or pecans
- 3 tbsp of rolled oats
- 1 tbsp melted vegan butter
- 2 tbsp light brown sugar, combined

Equipment: **large mixing bowl, medium and small bowls, hand or standing mixer, large spoon, whisk, parchment paper, aluminum foil, baking sheet, measuring cups & measuring spoons**

1. Preheat your oven to 350°F and line both of your baking sheets with parchment paper and set aside.
2. Wash your sweet potatoes, wrap in aluminum foil, place on parchment lined baking sheet, cover baking sheet with aluminum foil, then place in oven for 65–75 minutes or until completely tender (check with fork through center of largest potato).
3. Remove potatoes from oven and allow to cool (reduce cooling time by placing in fridge for 25 minutes or freezer for 15 minutes).
4. Once cooled, peel away potato skins, cube and place in large mixing bowl. Add all remaining ingredients (wet and dry) and combine with your mixer until smooth (do not overmix).
5. Now is the time to check for taste and consistency. If too thick, add a tablespoon or two of plant milk and combine. If not sweet sweet enough, add a tablespoon or two of agave and combine.
6. Pour filling evenly into your prepared pie crust, place aluminum foil around the edges of of the crust (to avoid burning), place on parchment lined baking sheet and bake for 30 minutes.
7. Remove from oven, add the topping evenly and bake another 25–30 minutes (If not using the topping, which is fine, bake straight through for about 60 minutes). Remove from oven, allow to cool and enjoy!

EVERYTHING COOKIES

25 MINS

$ $

The perfect post-workout or mid-day snack, this heavy-duty cookie will more than satisfy cookie connoisseurs of all ages in the house. It's a bit messy but loads of fun to make with the kids for a nice weekend family cookie party!

MAKES 35

- 1 ½ cups of vegan butter at room temperature
- ½ cup of unsweetened, unflavored applesauce
- 1 tbsp vanilla extract
- 3 cups of all purpose, unbleached flour
- 1 ½ cups organic cane sugar
- 1 ½ cups light brown sugar
- 1 tbsp baking powder
- 1 tbsp baking soda
- 1 tsp ground cinnamon
- ¼ tsp ground nutmeg
- 1 tsp kosher salt
- 3 cups of vegan chocolate chips
- 2 cups of unsweetened shredded coconut flakes
- 2 cups of raw walnuts, chopped
- 3 cups rolled oats

Equipment: large mixing bowl, medium and small bowls, hand or standing mixer, large spoon, whisk, parchment paper, baking sheets, measuring cups & measuring spoons

1. Preheat your oven to 350°F and line your baking sheets with parchment paper.
2. In a medium bowl, cream your butter with your mixer, then add both sugars and continue to mix until incorporated.
3. Add the vanilla extract and the applesauce, mix then set aside.
4. In a large bowl, add flour, baking soda, baking powder, salt and the spices and whisk to incorporate.
5. In a separate bowl, combine shredded coconut, walnut, chocolate chips and rolled oats and mix them together to combine and set aside.
6. Add the wet ingredients to the flour and spice mixture and mix on low until well combined.
7. With a spatula, fold in the blended coconut and oats mixture until it is well combined.
8. Make a round ball (somewhere between the size of a golf ball and a jumbo egg) and place on lined cookie sheet. Slightly flatten each cookie, place in oven and bake 13–15 minutes. Place on cooling rack and enjoy!

For cooking classes, food demos, lectures, exclusive HE products, speaking engagements or inquiries, go to herban-eats.com or send your query to info@herban-eats.com